D0500506

Not Your Mother's Midlife

Not Your Mother's Midlife

A Ten-Step Guide to Fearless Aging

Nancy Alspaugh
and Marilyn Kentz

Andrews McMeel Publishing
Kansas City

 For information, write Andrews McMeel Publishing, an Andrews McMeel Universal company, 4520 Main Street, Kansas City, Missouri 64111.

Library of Congress Cataloging-in-Publication Data

Alspaugh, Nancy.
Not your mother's midlife : a ten-step guide to fearless aging / Nancy Alspaugh and Marilyn Kentz.
p. cm.
Accompanied by a CD which provides the authors' "visualizations along with soothing music to help you achieve a relaxed state"—Introd.
Includes bibliographical references and index.
ISBN 0-7407-3524-1
1. Middle aged women—United States—Psychology. 2. Aging—United States—Psychological aspects. 3. Middle aged women—United States—Attitudes. 4. Self-esteem in women—United States. 5. Self-actualization (Psychology) I. Title: Midlife : a ten-step guide to fearless aging. II. Kentz, Marilyn. III. Title.

HQ1059.5.U5A47 2003
646.7'0084'4—dc21

2002045215

03 04 05 06 07 RDH 10 9 8 7 6 5 4 3

To our mothers,

LINA ASTI MATULICH and FRANCES ROUSSEAU ALSPAUGH

Who gave us lives filled with choices they didn't have.

We love you,
Marilyn and Nancy

Contents

Introduction

Not Your Mother's Midlife is more that just a book, it's a movement. It dares to challenge society's old, worn-out perception that women become less valuable as they age. If fact, it suggests that our mothers are the last generation to have to put up with that nonsense. Today's women can be more powerful, more capable, still desirable, and, most of all, happier as they age.

Four out of every ten American adults are baby boomers who have now become midlife bloomers. By sheer numbers we've got the edge, we've got the power, and we've got just enough therapy to kick this new attitude into gear! Aging is a hard pill for most women to swallow, but the two of us don't see it that way. We're proud of being middle-aged, and we're happier than we've ever been. Three years ago, however, we were both smack-dab in the middle of a midlife crisis. Nancy recalls, "My eight-year marriage was in shambles, I was struggling with infertility and remained childless, and I had reached a burnout point in my career in television with no idea of what I wanted to do next. I felt old, and though my friends couldn't understand why I wasn't appreciative enough of my youthful looks, I was a wreck on the inside, barely hanging on by a thread and my Paxil prescription."

Marilyn's life wasn't any better. "Three years ago my mom had suffered her first stroke, I had gained thirty unwanted pounds, my husband was an active alcoholic, and with three kids out the door and my baby daughter in high school, I was spiraling down into the empty-nest syndrome."

One night we found ourselves confiding in each other over a glass of wine. Marilyn: "We talked about our options. Nancy could have had an affair. I could have gotten liposuction . . . and then had an affair. I guess divorce was another option. But somehow we knew that things like that would simply cover up what was really bothering us deep down inside. We knew we had to look for the real reasons we were going for the antidepressants. Over the years we had both experienced a good amount of therapy, and both of us had followed many spiritual teachings and had gathered some good old-fashioned common sense. So we figured we had enough tools to help each other work on the most important part—the inside—and get out of this depression."

We decided to do something new: *create our own turning point.* Most of us think life hands us turning points. Think about the turning points that have affected you. How about when you met your first best friend? Got married? Had your first child? We have many turning points during our lifetimes—some good, and some not so good, like getting rejected by your first love. Some turning points come up unexpectedly—a car accident, for instance—and certainly September 11, 2001, was a huge turning point for our whole nation. What most of us don't understand is that we can create our own turning points. That night at dinner we made a conscious decision to stop feeling sorry for ourselves and help each other gain a more fulfilling life. We acknowledged that certain hardships automatically come with midlife—like aging parents, empty nests, and loose skin—and that we had better get ourselves ready for them. And we'd better find a way to change our perspectives.

Over the next two years we worked on projects and experimented to help us get in touch with what most women have to face once they turn forty. We were in new territory: awareness and decision making regarding getting old. We were grateful we had each other to conduct a reality check or two, and a hand to hold when it got hard. We discovered interesting ways to let go of what would inhibit a fulfilling second half of life and to focus on what would enhance it. Luckily for you, what took us three years to discover has now been condensed into a ten-week "Fearless Aging" plan.

Why title our book *Not Your Mother's Midlife*? We have nothing against our beloved moms—in fact, we dedicated this book to them. We are simply grateful that we are the lucky ones—we're the first generation of women who don't have to endure the fear of aging quietly and alone. We don't have to suffer, we don't have to be ashamed, and we don't have to lie if we don't want to. For our dear mothers there were no guidelines for being happy, healthy, glorious women once they reached a "certain age." Life for their generation was about being modest, frugal, and taken care of—something most of us know very little about. Our generation is made up of a variety of uninhibited women, from powerful executives to intelligent, creative stay-at-home moms, to those who tattoo their bums and believe a good credit card is the world's best nonprescription mood enhancer, to those who support themselves, their kids, and a few of the neighbors without the help of anyone.

Mom wasn't expected to go to college. She was supposed to live in her parents' home until she married, and to remain a virgin till her wedding night. Her virginity was almost guaranteed, because there was no Pill, and condoms were not sold in grocery stores or dispensed out of vending machines in bars. Those who did have a little fun often had to pay for it by marrying out of necessity instead of love, and most of those women stayed married because of the kids and the social pressure. Not our generation. We sent forth large groups of free-spirited women. A great number of us lived on our own right away, or communally, or with several different boyfriends, sequentially. And having babies was often put off in favor of a stimulating career, or by the confusion of having multiple sex partners.

When Mom was growing up, men ruled the house. First her father made all the decisions; later her husband set the family rules and doled out her weekly allowance. Her only power was over us kids, and even then some important tasks—like spanking—waited until Dad got home. By contrast, we call the shots; we set the parameters of what goes on in the house. That's not to say that there isn't still a community of women who have fallen right in line with their predecessors and even ask permission for a night out, but the majority of us buy, make, decorate, and wear the pants in the family.

In our mothers' world, feelings and family secrets were kept to yourself. There was no Jerry Springer, or even *Dateline,* for that matter, to publicize how bad off most of America really is. Psychologists were for those with extreme problems, group therapy was unheard of, and no one—repeat, *no one*—put on sold-out shows about their vagina!

Work (and, with it, outside stimulation and creative fulfillment) was mostly for the desperate and divorced. When she was single, if she was young and thin, a woman might have the opportunity to become a glamorous airline stewardess. Many women were secretaries before marriage but were expected to quit once they were "in a family way." If Mom did work, the one common choice was to be a teacher.

As time went by, the children, the house, the PTA, and the occasional family vacation to the Grand Canyon became the be-all and end-all of our mothers' social lives.

Mom lived for her family at the expense of herself. It was the natural, socially acceptable lifestyle. But it took its toll. Soon the lines in her face deepened, the kids rebelled and left, and the house was complete with whatever modest upgrades she could afford. What to do? She began her journey into midlife alone, and with no particular plan.

Compare her to the middle-aged woman of today who has a couple of in vitro–fertilized three-year-old twins in tow. In order to make the house payment she holds down a full-time job, and she lives plagued by guilt that she's hardly ever home. To this busy woman an empty nest just means the kids are messing with the damn birds in the backyard again.

Loneliness was a common liability for the average fifty-year-old of the past. Some filled their time with golf, gardening, charities, and bridge parties; for others, an affair put a spark in their egos and began the downfall of their marriages; and for even more women, Jim Beam and Merv Griffin became their only companions.

Well, this is not your mother's midlife. Lucky you! It's the twenty-first century, where a woman can do something creative with the second half of her life. Women can help each other with the hard stuff and begin to appreciate themselves in ways never before achieved. Welcome to the "Dry-Vagina Monologues"! Where you don't need a little red Mercedes or a new derriere to pick up your spirits, nor a lot of alcohol to numb your fears. All you need is a sense of perspective, a sense of humor, a couple of good friends, the willingness to do a little mental rearranging, and this book to show you how. We invite you to get a little militant about midlife and live it for all you're worth! It's time for the sisterhood of women to join arms, hold our I'm-worth-it/Miss Clairol heads high, and undergo a revitalization of the soul.

And it is a revitalization that is sorely needed at this frightening time in our lives. After the epic tragedy that hit our country on September 11, 2001, women (and men) began questioning their long-held values and belief systems. Knowing that our lives could end so brutally and suddenly seemed to shock us into a new reality overnight. Self-indulgent concerns about aging paled in comparison to the suffering we witnessed. We realized we are lucky to be alive and gained a new appreciation for what we do have. American women everywhere expressed a desire to be of service, to be useful, to make a difference in this lifetime. We want to contribute in a more deeply personal way, to go beyond giving money, donating blood, and waving our flag. Women can start to make a difference right now. It's not too late; in fact, it may be only the beginning. We can start by using our collective feminine powers to create instead of destroy, to nurture instead of criticize, and to become brave and courageous instead of scared. And we can certainly stop being self-absorbed, at least enough so that we won't let a few little wrinkles or the extra pounds that come with age get in the way of a potentially remarkable, satisfying life.

As you read these pages be aware that right now you have some choices. You can 1) try to ignore that you are in fact in midlife until you finally trip over your loose skin or your dead husband and simply fall into the old crisis mode; 2) have a doctor pull that skin real tight, memorize the latest P. Diddy tune, carry around never-to-be-used tampons, pierce something, and pretend you're young; or 3) join our Fearless Aging Club and create your own turning point. You can face midlife head-on, optimistic with the knowledge that you have the capability to make the rest of your life whatever you want it to be and that you don't have to do it alone.

The following ten turning points will help you face midlife with confidence and a positive attitude. Each corresponding chapter contains personal-growth exercises, humorous and poignant stories so that you'll see you're not alone, questions to stimulate you, and guided visualizations to help firm up your new way of thinking.

Turning Points at Midlife

1. Accept It If you are between the ages of forty and sixty you are in the middle of your life. You are middle-aged. You are in midlife. Before you turn this into a crisis, take solace in the notion that millions of other women are choking this truth back right now—just like you. It's going to be all right. If you accept this fact of life, you will have taken the first step to creating a fulfilling second half. And we're here to help.

2. Take a Good Look at What to Expect Once you embrace your biological age, you must take a good look at what to expect in the next few years, so that you can make healthy choices about how you want to handle it. We need to circle the wagons as we begin to lose our estrogen, our ova, our hair, our role as Mom, and our role as daughter. This chapter touches on the changes coming our way—both the good and the hard ones—and gives you tools for dealing with it.

3. Let Go of What's Not Working After forty years, it's likely you've seen patterns of your own behavior that benefit your well-being and some that work against you. Instead of continuing on the same old course until you die, we're suggesting that you take inventory now and use this new awareness to make the kinds of changes that will release you from old, trouble-making conduct. This chapter is designed to help you move past those problems and behaviors you've been hanging on to and shows you how to release them, opening the door to a satisfying second half of your life.

4. Shore Up Spiritually As we are pressed to face the highs and lows of the second half of life, one sustaining force that can give us comfort and courage is our spirituality. Having none can cause the uneasy sense of free-falling.

To shore up spiritually means to put in place that belief system, that ritual, that philosophy which speaks to your soul. It's our individual attempt to give and receive comfort, to make sense of what life has given us, and to aid in the effort to make the world a better place.

5. Get a New Perspective Think of your life as a tapestry woven with colorful memories. Keep in mind all the unique things that you've brought with you to this point. Nobody else has the background, the smile lines, the education, the hurtful memories, the joyous moments you do, and every little variation is what makes you distinctive.

The way we perceive our life plays a part in determining how we feel about the future. This recommendation helps you take a second look at yourself and appreciate who you are today.

6. Find a New Passion A fascinating woman in midlife is full of passion. Not the lusty, sexual kind of passion (well, sometimes that, too) but passion for something that takes her to new limits. Discovering a new passion or rekindling an old one will take the "crisis" right out of anyone's midlife and will make you an interesting person. And by the way, there's nothing sexier than a passionate woman! This chapter helps you find something that will turn you on more than a hot-fudge sundae.

7. Don't Just Vent . . . Reinvent Midlife is a perfect time to reinvent yourself, because if you don't, life will do it for you. Empty nest? Boring job? Stale marriage? Don't sit around eating bon-bons and complaining. Change! This chapter contains fascinating stories from women who had the courage to change.

8. Make New Goals With your new acceptance and awareness, you'll find that it's time to set new goals. Goals for the forty-something or fifty-something woman. This is an exercise not in simple New Year's resolutions but life-altering, fulfilling goals. What do you want to be doing in five years? Ten? We'll take you through several activities that will help you get connected to some significant, personal future plans, as well as to realize them.

9. Get a Coach One woman alone can be hardworking and tenacious; two women with the same intention will create power. With the support of like-minded women we can achieve almost anything. We'll show you how professional life coaches get action from their sedentary clients.

10. Awaken to the Muse Have a champion, and become someone's champion. The women you admire can offer an important insight into the woman you are capable of becoming. They can also provide you with a source of inspiration and encouragement, serving as a reminder of the possibilities that are out there when we work to achieve a dream. Conversely, becoming someone else's muse will give you a wonderful, new, irresistible perspective.

Not Your Mother's Tools

By using the tools provided in this book on a regular basis you can have accelerated support in replacing old behavior patterns with new ones.

Keep the following tips in mind as you work through each chapter.

How Your Friends Can Help

It starts with one good friend. Someone who, like most of us, needs a little perspective, support, and comfort; someone who wants nothing but the best for you, too. Ask her if she wants to try something new with you. See if she will lovingly and playfully go through this workbook with you. Maybe you can gather a couple of women you know and love, or perhaps want to know and love, and create your own Fearless Aging Club.

Who could Mom turn to in midlife if she wanted to set new goals or find a new passion? She got together with her female friends and confided her hopes and dreams in between items of gossip. Our mothers had the right idea of forming a women's group and supporting one another, even if they had to hide it under the guise of "a bridge club" or "quilting bee."

Today's woman can get all kinds of professional support, but even with all of our choices there's nothing like a good friend to help inspire us. And we don't have to pretend to be quilting if we don't want to—we can openly and proudly form our own Fearless Aging Club.

Make it official; give your group a name (have fun with that!) and stick to a meeting schedule. A strong support system will help you put the ideas contained in this book into action. Make it an experience you share. Maybe you can start off with a "Not Your Mother's Slumber Party." Or perhaps you can kick it off with a weekend retreat and book reading at an affordable spot or a friend's home where you can get away from the demands of job and family. Whatever you do, the most important thing is to meet every week—preferably in person, but at least by phone or e-mail.

Cover a chapter a week, reading through once on your own, then doing the exercises together. Designate one of the women as each week's official "life coach." Her job will be to organize the meeting, act as the facilitator, keep to a time schedule, and make sure everyone is heard. Or, if everyone prefers, one woman can be the facilitator for all of the ten weeks you are reading the book. The meetings can be held the same place each week, but it's also fun to switch houses, as well.

Of course, you can do the work contained in the book on your own. Our Web site, www.Fearless-Aging.com, is set up with a chat room so that you can join other women whose goals are the same as yours.

We find that the best way to turn any new thought into a belief system is through the strength we find when other women believe in us. Keep one another accountable, and if you fall behind in a goal, help each other determine what's blocking you.

Other Tools

Several other readily available resources can enable us to take the driver's seat and help us change our reality. Devices like guided visualization, self-talk, and affirmations have been used since the beginning of time. They're still around because they work. Aging hippies and enlightened New Age seekers practice these techniques regularly, but don't worry—if you start using these tools as part of your daily ritual, you won't be tempted to let the hair under your arms grow out. Just think of it as another form of prayer.

Questions

Throughout the book we will pose some thought-provoking questions. They're simply meant to entice you into the world of self-exploration. Write your answers in a journal, and—if you feel comfortable—share some of your insights with your group. Keep writing past your initial response to discover what buried thoughts you carry. These impressions might be only slightly related to that first reaction. When you've finished, without judgment, see what new and interesting aspect of yourself you've learned about. Then make a conscious choice as to which way you plan to move forward. You may say to yourself, "I don't need to keep this old belief—it does me no good" and program yourself for something new. Or you may discover something wonderfully unique about yourself that you want to nurture.

If You Can Imagine It, You Can Create It

Creative visualization is a wonderful and relaxing tool that gets you closer to your goal of happiness. We've provided you with a CD that contains our original visualizations, along with soothing music to help you achieve a relaxed state. The CD supplies the imagery; all you have to do is relax and soak it in.

When your mind can put you in the setting of your goal, so that you're feeling the sensations and opening up your emotions, it will accommodate you later on when you try to make this goal into reality. When you're ready, and whether you prefer to be with friends or alone, be sure to do this exercise at a time when you won't be interrupted. Turn off the phone and choose a quiet, relaxed environment. You'll begin by taking some deep breaths. If you hear cars passing, dogs barking, or children playing, give yourself the suggestion that these outside sounds will help to relax you. You may sit up comfortably or lie down on the floor. However, it is not recommended to do your creative visualizations on your bed, where you might be tempted to fall asleep.

It's our goal to give you this wake-up call and help you become as happy and powerful as you are meant to be. To revel in fearless aging. To begin to nurture who you really are, bunions and all, and embrace the second half of your life with courage and excitement.

Now, grab a couple of girlfriends and begin.

Not Your Mother's Midlife

Chapter One

Turning Point No. 1: Accept It

YOUR MOTHER'S MIDLIFE: *For our mothers' generation, acceptance meant resignation—resigning oneself to becoming old in an appropriate, acceptable fashion. Midlife meant it was time to cut and perm her hair. If she was married with children, she was dealing with the empty-nest syndrome and anticipating the role of grandmother. If she wasn't married, she settled into "spinsterhood," becoming known as an "old maid." She was instructed never to tell anyone her real age.*

YOUR MIDLIFE: *For you, acceptance means celebration! With a little courage we can admit how old we are openly and proudly. "Old maid" has been converted to "happily single," and grandmother may be one of the many roles we take on in this phase, the time of our lives.*

If you are between the ages of forty and sixty you are in the middle of your life. You are middle-aged. You are in midlife. Say it: *Midlife, midlife, midlife.* Now, before you turn it into some kind of crisis, take a deep breath and relax, knowing that millions of other women are trying to hide from this truth right now—just like you. You are not alone. It's going to be all right. We'll be with you all the way. If you accept this fact of life, you will have taken the first step to creating a fulfilling second half. Keep reading.

Bond with those who share your struggle. Look each other squarely in the eyes and say, "We're getting old . . . so what?" Then laugh about it, or cry together. Just don't ditch your peers by thinking something foolish like "Well, you may be getting old, but I'm getting tucked!" No amount of lying, silicone, or Botox will change the fact that underneath it all you are still forty-five or fifty-five or sixty-five. Before you can begin to celebrate midlife, you must own up to the fact that you are in it.

It's not easy. We try to overlook the upper arms as long as we can. We fear crossing the line to . . . ailments. Here's Marilyn's first peek into her middle-aged reality.

BUNIONS

I was in denial. My foot was in so much pain, but I couldn't face it. Bunions were something old ladies had. It wasn't until I had to pass up a very cute pair of Nine West shoes for something "bunion-friendly" that I knew it had to be removed. Embarrassed about my condition, I refused to call it by its name. To avoid the B word, I just said I needed a "foot operation."

While my doctor was examining my throbbing foot he asked me if I was allergic to any drugs. The conversation naturally drifted to the hippie era of the sixties. Turns out my podiatrist had been at Woodstock and I had been at Altamont—the concert where the Hell's Angels killed somebody (only I didn't notice, but that's another story). As I lay on the examining table, I mentioned how odd it was to be discussing counterculture "happenings" with the man who was about to remove my bunion. Never in a million years would I have thought that such "hip flower children" would be doing such geezerly things.

Push Through It

Remember: You are not alone in your struggle. You belong to a generation of people who are doing the same thing that you are at this very moment. Each generation is unique unto itself. Yes, you may no longer be in with the "in crowd," but if you lose respect for your own age group, you will in essence be turning your back on yourself. Run with your own in crowd.

Each generation separates itself from the one before, in a rite of passage that begins when we're in our teens. With this detachment comes group pride. Can you remember being sixteen and thinking, "Our generation has more soul, more compassion, more understanding of the way the world should be"? Adolescence is the time in our life when we are the hip ones. We are the taut ones. We are critical of our parents and all they stand for. And we begin to separate ourselves from them. This is appropriate behavior for sixteen-year-olds. It is as it should be.

But somewhere in our thirties some of us observe that our friends and neighbors appear to be following in the footsteps of our dorky parents. We withdraw from them and form a subgroup that tries to infiltrate the "now generation." We fear the worst: becoming our mother. Next thing you know, we think, we'll be wearing a visor that matches our culottes.

Maybe some of us could get away with posing as one of the young hotties when we were in our thirties, but with each passing year it becomes harder and harder to hide the stretch marks peeking out of the limited fabric in that trendy new outfit.

And so we must exfoliate. And tuck the excess skin. Now, don't misunderstand—there's nothing wrong with getting a little plastic surgery. However, it's no exaggeration when we tell you that we know women who have gone way beyond the usual cut-and-paste we all fantasize about, to a world where the term *hand job* refers not to pleasuring one's partner but to the plastic surgery that gives her hands a youthful look. "Elbow lifts" are equally as popular, and the most desperate are dyeing what's left of their pubic hair and even getting a "vaginal tuck."

What exactly causes women to panic like this? Let's get to the bottom of it. Are we worried that we'll lose our ability to stir lust in the opposite sex? Is the need to be sexy so ingrained in our psyches that we'd rather spend our hard-earned money erasing age spots than exploring the world? That must be why some of us miss a house payment to buy that cute little red sports car (yes, plenty of women do that, too), hoping that some buffed male thing will notice the vaginal tuck as we race by.

However, what you choose to do to your body—whether it's

applying mascara or having a neck lift—is your business. And it doesn't mean you can't age fearlessly if you look like a cat. We recognize that women will always want to look attractive. How far you go is your choice. As long as you are taking good care of the inside, it doesn't matter which way your face grows old.

Consider this for one tiny moment: Let us love and appreciate youth—it's their turn. And let's remember that there's a middle ground between youth and the elderly. We belong to an important club made up of people who carry the same fears, memories, and struggles as we do. People who dye the gray out of their hair, worry about their children, mourn their aging parents, wonder if Botox will give them mad-cow disease, and are finally old enough to appreciate a beautiful sunset . . . without pot. Why would we want to ditch them? They are our support system. They are our link with our reality.

Sometimes it's a shock how much time has gone by. Little reminders come at odd times. If we pay attention to these reminders, we can stay in the world of acceptance. Here's one that shocked Marilyn:

> I was watching *Saturday Night Live* last year, and when guest host The Rock introduced the band AC/DC, I thought, "Hmmmm, not my era. I think they were popular during the years I spent on the bleachers at the Little League games. Yep, I'm a little too old for AC/DC." Then it hit me. Wait a minute—these guys are geezers!
>
> Look, I've gotten used to the ancient Rolling Stones, Elton John's toupee, and Billy Joel's paunch, but when I saw AC/DC's lead guitar player with wrinkled knees and thinning, wispy long hair writhing around on the floor, I thought he was having a Parkinson's moment. Was that supposed to be a groovy move? What may have been this guy's "thing" to turn on the young ones in the eighties now looked like he might be wetting himself. I repeat—and this is the hard part—I'm older than he is. I have medication in my bathroom drawer that could help this

guy. And just the other day someone told me the Beastie Boys are pushing forty.

What a trip!

Sometimes it's a shock, but we must face it. And don't think it's not hard work. The first time a young shoe clerk calls you ma'am, you'll want to slap him. When a Gap sales clerk mistakes your best friend for your daughter, you'll want to jam your trendy high heel into his face. Resist it. Push through it. You can handle it. Mother Nature's not some kind of hit man (okay, woman). Mother Nature's not completely cruel. She doesn't give it to us all at once. We don't wake up one fine morning and all of a sudden our ass has hit rock bottom. She's compassionate enough to age us in little spurts. Marilyn is reminded of the first time she couldn't flirt her way out of a traffic ticket:

> I was so used to turning on my "cute charm" to get myself out of those kinds of little predicaments that when the twenty-something officer who pulled me over had no response, I was taken aback. A little nervous that I might have lost my youthful charm, I poured it on a little thicker . . . and yet he kept writing out the damn ticket. I had nothing left to do but pull out the tears. Even then he must have seen me as a pathetic Joan Collins, because he actually yawned as he handed it to me.

Nancy was window-shopping in New York City when she realized that something had changed:

> About four years ago I was in New York. I had just gotten out of an important meeting where I had kicked ass and I was feeling good! I took long strides in my handsome suit and cool shoes. I was wearing a big "I just kicked ass" grin. The two young blondes in skimpy outfits walking directly in front of me didn't notice my power gate. Actually, neither did anyone else. I realized with a shock that every man that passed us was ogling the

> fresh ones and looking right past me! I felt invisible. I ran home, got out my bottle of Clairol, and put on a short skirt!

No, acceptance doesn't come easy, but come it must. Linda, a fifty-two-year-old friend of ours, was reluctantly getting her annual Pap smear from a new gynecologist, fifteen years her junior. As the young doctor was prying her legs apart she demanded, "Does your mother know you're doing this?"

Ellen tells of a time when she was watching a football game on television. She was admiring the players with the mind-set of a young woman. "He's really cute" and "He's hot," she was thinking, when it suddenly dawned on her that she could have given birth to any and all of those husky men.

And as Nancy knows, when the reproductive system lets us down, it can be a difficult road to acceptance:

> I just assumed my eggs would always be in plentiful supply, like the grade AA large in the cartons at the grocery store. Then my fertility doctor explained that starting at about the age of thirty-seven, human eggs become rarer and rarer, and they become harder and harder to fertilize, until sometime in your mid- to late forties they simply dry up! Dry up? I thought, "This can't be happening to me—I never even used my good eggs!" In fact, I had spent years trying to keep my good eggs from becoming fertilized.
>
> It was a real shock to realize that there was something beyond my control. I had always been able to control everything around me by simply working harder, like so many career-obsessed women of the eighties and nineties. I attacked my first in vitro attempt at the age of thirty-nine much the same way I would have tackled producing a television show: I did everything the doctor told me to do and then some. I awaited the results of the pregnancy test, assuming success, as I would have assumed good ratings or a good review. I simply wasn't expecting to hear "Your results are negative."

Suddenly, my age was betraying me. Of course, I thought I could control that fact as well. Nature simply didn't intend for my body, in its mid-forties state, to reproduce any longer. But hell, there are plenty of other things that nature didn't intend for me to do after the age of forty—like wear a bikini—that I do anyway. Only this was a whole new ball game. To accomplish my goal, I would first have to accept the fact that I would be flying in the face of Mother Nature, and could be in for a long and arduous challenge. And that it was.

In all cases Mother Nature rules. Don't be alarmed. Seek out someone who understands. Please note: Reconnecting with your own generation doesn't mean you get rid of the younger friends you have, nor does it mean you should call all your old pals from Poughkeepsie High. It just means that it's time you feel a sense of pride and respect about who you are and how old you are. And it helps if you can laugh about it with someone who knows exactly what you're going through. With honesty comes laughter. And with laughter comes closeness and support of the real you.

Creative Visualization: Good Enough

(NUMBER ONE ON CD)

The following visualization will help release the part of you that supports the limited belief that youth is the key to achieving love and acceptance from others. It encourages you to give a gentle good-bye to youth and prompts you to appreciate who you are today.

Get into a comfortable position, either sitting in a chair, cross-legged on the floor, or lying down. Close your eyes. Begin to inhale through your nostrils and exhale through your mouth, gradually intensifying the deepness of your breath. With each inhalation, expand your stomach and chest, filling your lungs with air, and with each exhalation, empty your breath from your chest and stomach until they feel "collapsed." Do this very slowly. Breathe in through your nose to the count of four, hold your breath to the count of seven, then slowly exhale from your mouth to the count of eight. With each new breath imagine yourself pulling in positive energy and everything you need, and with each exhalation feel yourself letting go of negativity and everything you don't need in your life. Do this several times.

Imagine yourself as an adult looking at a ten-year-old little girl. The child looks just like you did when you were ten. In fact, it is you at ten. Look at her. What is she wearing? What does her hair look like? What is she doing? Ask her who her friends are. Take time to listen to her answer. Ask her what makes her happy. What are her concerns? Her hopes? Her dreams? Her fears? Is there anything special you want to say to her? Any advice you want to give her? If so, do it now. Look directly into her eyes, put your hands on her shoulders, and say, "You're good enough just the way you are." Give her a hug and tell her good-bye.

Now see yourself as you were at eighteen. See this teenager through your adult eyes. What is she wearing? What does her hair look like? What is she doing? Who are her friends? What makes her happy? What are her concerns? Her hopes? Her dreams? Her fears? Is there anything you want to say to her? Any advice? If so, do it now. Look directly into her eyes, put your hands on her shoulders, and say, "You're good enough just the way you are." Give her a hug and tell her good-bye.

Now visualize your twenty-five-year-old self. Take a good look at this young woman. What is she wearing? What is she doing? Who are her friends? What makes her happy? What are the hopes of this twenty-five-year-old you? Her dreams? Her fears? Is there anything special you want to say to her? If so, do it now. Look directly into her eyes, put your hands on her shoulders, and say, "You're good enough just the way you are." Give her a hug and tell her good-bye.

Next look at the thirty-nine-year-old you. She's about to turn forty. What is she wearing? What does her hair look like? What is she doing? Who are her friends? What makes her happy now? What are her concerns? Her hopes? Her dreams? Her fears? Is there anything you want to say to her? If so, do it now. Look directly into her eyes, put your hands on her shoulders, and say, "You're good enough just the way you are." Give her a hug and tell her good-bye.

Now see yourself at your present age. Who are your friends? What makes you happy? What are your concerns, your hopes, your dreams, your fears? Is there anything you want to say to yourself? If so, do it now . . . then say, "You're good enough just the way you are."

You come upon a door. Beyond that door is a wonderful, creative, satisfying future. When you're ready, put your hand on the doorknob and walk across the threshold. Take a nice deep breath. Look around. What are some of the things you see? A beautiful home, a fulfilling, nurturing workplace? You hear the voices of happy people. Who could they be? Take it all in—this wonderful world you've created. Enjoy the view and spend a little time soaking in this new environment.

In a moment you are going to come back to the present, feeling relaxed and refreshed. Begin by taking three deep breaths. Notice the outside sounds. Start to wiggle your fingertips and your toes. Breathing regularly, open your eyes.

Share

Whether you did this visualization with a partner or with your support group, it's important to take some time to share what you just experienced. If you did it alone, it's still good to process what you just learned about yourself. Write about it in a journal and revisit it in a week or two.

Pay attention to some of the symbols that may have come up during the visualization, not only when you went through the door but also with each era you visited. A certain sweater, a hair ribbon, or an obscure friend could have a special meaning to the person who sees them. If you're processing the visualization in a group, ask each person what each symbol means to them.

It's not uncommon for tears to come up during this visualization. If that happened, explore what the tears are about. Compassion? Nostalgia? Sadness?

There will be some people who won't see anything when they open the door. Understand that whatever you encounter is what you are ready to look at.

If at any time you experience uncomfortable anxiety, use that as a message from your subconscious that this may be a "hot" issue for you. It may be something you could explore further with a trusted professional therapist, counselor, or member of the clergy.

QUESTION

The following question is for you to explore on paper. You don't have to reveal your innermost thoughts to anyone if you don't wish to. Remember to write past your initial response to reveal what's underneath. It doesn't matter how shallow or ridiculous your answer may seem—just keep writing.

What's holding you back from fully enjoying your true age?

When you're finished writing, note whether you already happen to be implementing any actions that address any of these fears. For example, if you worry that you'll have a stroke, do you eat healthful foods or exercise regularly? If you fear boredom, do you have a plan? For now, just explore the fears and your behaviors. Awareness alone is a powerful tool. In later chapters, we'll work on planning for a better future.

~

One fun way to embrace your generation is to celebrate each meaningful decade with your peers. Turning forty is the first of the big parties. You'll find that your general party stores gladly provide all the over-the-hill paper goods you'll ever need, Hallmark has plenty of "You're so old you can't remember squat" cards to provide the laughs, and the cliché "no spring chicken" will be overheard as the birthday girl passes the watercooler at work. Don't fight it; celebrate it. Glorify it with those of your own kind. Marilyn tells of two inventive ways to commemorate the passing into a new decade.

THE PROM RIDE

The first "big" party I celebrated was with four of my "ya-ya" friends from high school in November 1987; we had all turned forty sometime that year. The idea was to spend an evening in our hometown going down memory lane together. We each saved up for months so we could rent a limo; then we dressed in our old prom gowns (some of us had to insert a big panel down the back), teased our hair all the way to heaven, sprayed it rock hard with Aqua Net, crowned it with a tiara, and slathered our lips with heaps of white lipstick. We looked like the real thing. I saw my image reflected in the mirror and thought, "Isn't it ironic? When it was finally our turn to wear lipstick . . . the popular color was white. The funny thing is, I'm still wearing that same lipstick today . . . under my eyes!"

That night we were each responsible for providing one surprise "memory spot" to which the limo would take us. As we uncorked the first bottle of champagne, Vicki handed the driver an envelope. First place: Montecito Heights—the old make-out spot. As we drove up the winding hill we laughed at all the memories that began spilling out. Years ago we'd had a point system that we used when double-dating. Five points meant there was mild kissing going on. Ten (which would be used in a code sentence such as "Gee, my dad wanted me home by *ten*"), meant French-kissing. Now, fifteen points was a little tricky. Fifteen meant the guy was feeling you up. I told them about my special way of getting my fifteen points and still saving my reputation (which actually meant something in 1964). I would pretend I was sound asleep. I'd let my date cop a little feel, then wake up in shock. "How could you?! Oh no! You got the whole bra off and everything! You cad!" This ruse worked only on the slower boys. The next level was twenty points, for dry-humping—my favorite. And the most points one could get was twenty-five—going all the way! Back in 1964, a young girl did not go all the way; that is, unless of course you were a Catholic girl. I don't know which Catholic girl Billy Joel was singing about, but it certainly wasn't any of the ones I went to school with. Oh, come on, how many of us went to school with someone who had to drop out because of "mononucleosis"? Think about it—she was a Catholic girl, right?

While we were parked and reminiscing up on Make-out Mountain, Vicki had another little surprise for us. She had hired a couple of policemen to pretend to bust us. With their flashlights glaring in my eyes, I found myself panicking for a split second that my parents were gonna kill me. Then, as I remembered that it was thirty-three years later and that I had actually done a lot worse things in my twenties, I calmed down, and the champagne and tears of laughter once again began to flow.

Next it was Cheryl's turn to hand the limo driver her envelope.

We found ourselves in front of her old house. Back in '65 this was where all the wild slumber parties took place. We would run around her house in our baby-doll pajamas with our hair gooped up with Dippity-Do and wrapped around orange-juice cans. After stealing booze from her dad's bar, we would call boys on her pink Princess phone with The Beatles' "Help" playing in the background in stereophonic sound.

As we ran up her walkway, Cheryl explained to us that though she had meant to contact the current owners of the house, she never had gotten around to doing it. So there we stood: five forty-year-old women in prom dresses and tiaras with Cheryl's gloved finger poised on the doorbell. You can imagine the look on the faces of the nice older couple as we begged for a tour. They were in the middle of watching *Dallas* and were kind (or stupid) enough to let us tear through their house while they went back to their program.

Then it was my turn to reveal a surprise. There was this guy we'd all dated and fought over all those years ago. He'd been a real flirt in high school and had been renowned for having the best "Johnny Mathis make-out parties" in town. Not one of us had seen him since the old days. Before our reunion, I'd done a little research, contacted him, and arranged for him to meet us at his parents' house. As the limo wound its way through the familiar streets, my tipsy girlfriends began to squeal.

"*No!* We're not going to *his* house, are we?"

"OH . . . MY . . . "

"GOD!"

With complete glee they began to preen themselves, each prom queen fighting for mirror space. We rounded the final corner and saw a figure standing on the front lawn. We could almost hear Johnny Mathis's "Chances Are" floating out from his screen door between screams of teenage egos.

"Is that *him*? Is that *him*?"

"No! That's his *father*!"

"No, it's HIM!"

There stood our date. Fat and bald. But that image lasted only seconds, until our memories overwhelmed us. Soon all we could see was the cute surfer boy that once was. He had a corsage for each one of us. We giggled and swooned when he asked each of us for a dance, his parents peeking out from the window.

We returned to our coach and as we headed to the next destination, we revealed to one another how many points each one of us had gotten with him back in 1964. I swear some people exaggerated!

My favorite place of surprise that night came from the most popular one of us all: Vanessa Devoto. When I was in high school I wanted more than anything to be a song leader. I was like any girl that age: lonely, frightened, and desperately wanting to belong. I thought that if I were a song leader, I would finally be good enough. I would finally be worth something. I put extra effort into the tryouts. I stressed out about it, lost sleep over it, lost hair over it. I overrehearsed my kicks, my tricky moves, and my enthusiastic smile.

I didn't make it. I lost. I was absolutely devastated. And my mother didn't have the courtesy to hire a hit man.

That night a big football game was being played between the two rival high schools. When the limo pulled up to Baily Field I almost died. We got out, followed Vanessa down onto the field, and when she cued the band, we ripped the pompoms out of those little cheerleaders' hands and began to cheer. And the crowd roared. Okay, half the crowd roared. The other half was saying, "What are those old ladies doing on our field?"

Magic was created that night. A kind of magic that mixed memories, wild costumes from our own era, and creative surprises—a magic that, by the way, can be shared only with those of the same generation.

~

Reminiscing about your youth (without getting hung up on it) can keep you in a proud place regarding your peers. When Katerina, forty-seven, recalls her favorite era she is reminded of the close bond with her female friends:

> It's easy to accept my era—it was such a good one. Whenever I see any of my friends from the sixties we fall back into proudly reminiscing about the times we made Indian food, read poetry, swam naked, and demonstrated. We read *The Second Sex* and *Fear of Flying,* we took the Pill and responsibility for our own orgasms, we got married, had kids, got divorced, went to therapy, recycled, broke the glass ceiling, and even tried to take Yoko Ono seriously. Crazy as it was, most of us managed to pull through and succeed. We saw ourselves as the best and the brightest, but there was also a sense that we were part of a community. It was as if all of us, all of these women, magically knew the words to the same song and could sing in harmony. I can still hear the song.

QUESTIONS

What is unique about your generation?

What makes you proud to be a part of that generation?

ACTIVITY: Reason to Be Proud

List some of the contributions for which your generation is known. For example: Are you a part of the generation that carries high work ethics? Created rock 'n' roll? Taught our sons it's okay to cry and our daughters to be assertive? Has a new outlook on how to treat the dying?

When you put your mind to it, you have many reasons to be

proud of your generation. And your pride might be quite different than anyone else's. It's fun to see what others have learned from life. Write your ideas about your unique generation on the lines below.

Now, get together with your study group and brag!

Celebrate It Big, Celebrate It Creatively

Okay, the fiftieth party is huge. But it's not just about having a party to celebrate your collective birthdays. It's about finding an outlet to nurture female bonding and bring out the creativity in each of us. It's best to arrange something where all those invited have to contribute to the celebration in their own unique way. It takes a little more planning on everyone's part, and in the end all are richer for having done so.

Marilyn invites you to take a page from her book when it comes to throwing a fiftieth bash:

> When it was time to celebrate our entry into our fifties, the ya-yas reunited, this time for a weekend of mania at my house in Los

Angeles. The theme was "Seven Decades of Fun," and each one of us dressed in a different outfit that represented every decade we had been living on this earth, starting with the forties.

Late that Friday afternoon the ya-yas arrived at LAX dressed to kill in their costumes. I got Brian Peck, a close friend of mine who'll do anything in the name of fun, to pick up my cohorts. He was dressed up like a doctor. None of them had ever met Brian before, so they were a little confused. He drove them to my house, where he told them to wait at the front door, which I had decorated with yards of pink satin to resemble our mothers' vaginas. Meanwhile, he came in by way of the side door, grabbed my kitchen tongs, and, with Benny Goodman playing in the background, proceeded to "deliver" each one into my house. He slapped their butts, and the party began!

Barbara represented the year we were born—1947. She wore a belted suit with shoulder pads and sported a hat with netting over her eyes à la Joan Crawford.

I was the fifties girl, but instead of the typical poodle skirt, I wore my old uniform from St. Eugene's Elementary School. Well, not the exact one. I called the uniform company and told them I had a daughter entering the sixth grade who was rather large for her age and did they happen to have a uniform in size fourteen? I was in luck. With my white buck shoes and bobby sox, and carrying my rosary beads, I looked just like I did in 1957 . . . only with gray roots near my ponytail. My contribution that evening was brown-bag lunches that contained each person's favorite sandwich from our school days. There were two tunas, one peanut butter and jelly, three salamis, and a bologna . . . all on Wonder Bread and wrapped up in waxed paper. I threw in chips, Hostess Sno Balls, and little cartons of milk.

Yvonne didn't have to do too much to transform herself into an icon from the sixties—though it had been quite a while since I'd seen the old fringed-and-beaded leather vest over that tie-dyed T-shirt. With her protest sign firmly in one hand and a doobie in the other, she was ready for anything. As a matter of fact, her contribution could have gotten us in jail. We had Dr. Brian, our designated driver, take us to Hollywood Boulevard, where Yvonne handed each of us a protest sign, a bra, and a book of matches. My goodness, that cotton and polyester catches quick. People were driving by honking and cheering, but since it was Hollywood, burning things was no big deal.

Marsha wore go-go boots and a white wig. She looked like she'd come out of a door on *Laugh-In*. Before we left the house she had a fashion show of all her clothes from the seventies. Can you imagine saving a pink-and-orange psychedelic flower-power shift?

Vicki was an exact copy of Jennifer Beals in *Flash Dance,* torn sweatshirt, leg warmers, and all. She took us to a disco, where we danced to the likes of Donna Summer and the Bee Gees. I don't know if we got winded from dancing or from laughing, but after a while we had to sit down. We ended up in the back room reminiscing and cracking up about our afflictions, of all things. Each one was trying to top the other with a more serious ailment story. Vicki is an ovarian-cancer survivor, Marsha was in a terrible car accident, and Yvonne has a pacemaker. Feeling a little left out, Cheryl tried to top them all by bragging, "Well, I had a grande mal seizure!"—which made us burst into uncontrollable laughter. I know it sounds strange to be joking about such tragic and awful things, but when you get together with dear old friends, it's easy to get on a roll where anything and everything is funny.

The party took place in 1997, and since she was representing the nineties, Cheryl simply dressed normally. We went back to my house, said good-bye to Brian, poured ourselves a nightcap, and got in the hot tub. Naked. You want to feel good about yourself? Get naked with a bunch of women your exact age. When you're fifty, even those who look great in absolutely anything have just as many natural flaws as the ones sitting next to her. So there we all sat, submerged in warm water, the light of a crescent moon gleaming off seven pairs of bobbing breasts, talking about the latest fad diet.

Vanessa represented the future so, dressed like a stereotypical "old lady" on her way to Las Vegas, she had us play the Gossip Game. She had created a trivia game about all our gossip and happenings over the years. We had to guess which one of us she was talking about. A few shocking surprises were revealed in the wee hours of the morning. By the light of dawn she pulled out a crystal ball and predicted a great, if hysterical, future for all of us.

The rest of the weekend was dedicated to eating, laughing, crying, and becoming even closer. It was so much fun—better than any vacation I've ever had.

When you turn forty, fifty, sixty, seventy, eighty, ninety and one hundred, grab your cronies and create your own special event. There's nothing else like it.

ACTIVITY: The Youngest Team Wins!

You may not be surprised how much of our world is youth oriented, but it might shock you how much we all buy into it.

Team up into pairs. With candid abandon, and without judgment, brainstorm with your partner about all the ways you try to appear younger. Include things as trite as wearing mascara and using teen slang such as "What's up?" Be frightfully honest and do this with a heavy dose of humor. Set the timer for ten minutes. The team with the longest list wins.

ACTIVITY: The Peer-Bonding Party

Invite five or so women who are in your approximate age group to a peer-bonding party. The invitations don't necessarily have to go to your old high school friends, just to any fun woman who is around your age. Ask each of them to bring their favorite song from sometime in their teens—and the memories to go with it. Encourage them to bring some photographs of themselves at the time "their song" was popular. You'll all get a kick out of seeing who was the preppy cheerleader, who was the intellectual, and who was the hippie chick. If you want, collect some clothes and accoutrements from that era and reminisce to the strains of "Nights in White Satin" or "Sugar Pie Honey Bunch" as you celebrate your past together.

~

Whether it's the embarrassment of new little wrinkles, wanting to date and feeling too old, or having no model for fearless aging, we hold on to youth like a security blanket. You cannot experience the thrill of liberating your true self unless you accept who you are today. Once you're honest about your biological age, you can be free. Midlife is extraordinary because you're no longer that lost adolescent and you don't yet have one foot in the grave. Give up worrying about the mistakes you made in your youth and let go of the fear of the aging process—this is truly the best time of your life, as good as it gets. Gather your generation and celebrate. Be grateful you've all made it to this point and rejoice in the possibility that, who knows, the best is yet to come . . . if you let it.

Chapter Two

Turning Point No. 2: Take a Good Look at What to Expect

YOUR MOTHER'S MIDLIFE: *For the most part, our mothers only had their own mothers' experiences to model what they could expect. It often looked like Mom was doomed to spend the second half of her life with Lawrence Welk nipping Geritol. If she took a good look at what lay ahead of her, she might have thought that aches and pain were all there was.*

YOUR MIDLIFE: *Just like childhood, adolescence, our twenties, and our thirties, midlife has a little of everything—a whole lot of good, some bad, and, well yeah, a little ugly, too! Luckily for our midlife, we can hold each other's hand while walking through the hard parts and celebrate with our new faces in the twenty-first century.*

Once you embrace your biological age, you must take a good look at what to expect in the years to come so that you can make some healthy choices about how you want to handle it. Pulling your head out of the sand empowers you.

There are plenty of misconceptions about middle age. Let's take a look at what's real. Some of this new adventure will be exhilarating and some devastating. This chapter is divided into two sections: "The Hard Stuff," which will give you insight about some of the realities we'd all like to avoid, and "The Good Stuff," which will give you a little appreciation for what's coming your way.

THE HARD STUFF

Let's take this head-on and start with the worst eventuality: death. Don't avoid these next few passages, because they are designed to prepare you for when (not if) it's your turn.

As you begin to enter into midlife, you will notice that death and illness seem to be popping up all around you. Suddenly everyone you know is dealing with an aging parent, or perhaps the loss of one, and cancer is as ubiquitous as the common cold. Pretty heavy stuff, when ten years ago the biggest problem on your mind was whether or not you would get that promotion you wanted. And not only are you caught off guard by this new unwanted passage of life but it seems as though it's visiting you in multiples, a tidal wave of doom. Should Dad go into assisted living? Will your sister need that mastectomy or will the chemotherapy be enough to destroy the cancer cells? Will your friend's husband have to have triple bypass surgery? Meanwhile, we try to make it through the little daily problems of life—the flat tires, idiot bosses, senile parents, and kids who keep pooping their drawers—with a good attitude. On top of all that, we are faced with this reality: You can run but you can't hide, because like a face-lift, denial goes only so far.

The most important and sustaining element that will help you throughout the rest of your life is friendship. Keep your good friends close to you—they will play the part of your mother and your soul sister. They will nurture you through the hell of the death of someone you love. This is the wonderful legacy our mothers have passed down to us. The strong bond of womanhood has been around since the beginning of time. Thank God.

Losing Our Mothers

The feelings a woman experiences with the death of her mother are almost unbearably strong. Whether your relationship was intimate or estranged, the loss of your mother is immense. Chris is fifty years old. She received some sage advice when her mom died at age seventy-one after a brief battle with leukemia. Chris was very close to her mom even though they lived far apart. What she learned from two of her mother's friends both is touching and will help us when it's our turn.

THE PHONE

The day after my mom died her neighbor Donna came over with some food and things. My kids always played with hers when we visited, so I'd gotten to know her pretty well. She loved my mom. That morning she apologized for not coming by more, saying that she was only just getting over her own mother's death from two years ago, and she felt that she couldn't handle it when my mom took a turn for the worse. She said, as I stood there with the waterworks going full tilt, "You know, I've never told anyone this, but after my mom died, I used to call the house and just let the phone ring. I would do it often. For some reason it made me feel better."

After many successful years of working, my mom had met her "white-haired ladies" while taking classes at the Y. She would tell me about how much fun they were, especially her new, very good friend Cheryl.

I finally met white-haired Cheryl at the wake. She and her phalanx of white-haired ladies were the very first to arrive. She blew into the room, took one look at me, and, with her arms open wide, said, "I loved your mother, I loved your mother, I loved your mother" as she gave me a huge hug. It was absolutely the right way to start the evening.

The next day she called to see how I was doing. Then she revealed her personal story: "Believe it or not, I know exactly how you're feeling. I was sixty when my mother died, and . . . I've never told anyone this . . . but I used to call her house and just let the phone ring. For some reason it just made me feel better."

Through my sobs I tried to tell her how amazing it was to hear that, and I told her about Donna, my mom's neighbor. She said,

"You're not really a grown-up until you can't call your mother on the phone anymore. You're a grown-up now, sweetie."

Finding the Courage

Real courage comes when life gives us an overdose of the hard stuff at once and we simply face it any way we can. It's noteworthy to recognize someone who makes it through the hardships with honor and courage. They usually see themselves as regular people just handling what God gives them—not doing anything special, just putting one foot in front of the other. They really don't see themselves as heroes. Maybe we could point it out to them once in a while. Marilyn gives us insight as she observes her close friend Vicki, fifty-five, facing three huge challenges at the same time:

> A couple of years ago Vicki's mother went from being an active seventy-five-year-old to an advanced Alzheimer's patient within a very short nine months; her father got hit by a golf cart and injured his hip, landing him in a convalescent home; and her husband was in the advanced stages of Parkinson's. At one point she would leave school after a long day of teaching six-year-olds, go visit her father for about a half an hour, drive across town to comfort her mother, then travel to a close but neighboring town to visit her husband. She would get home around nine-thirty, make herself dinner (which usually consisted of popcorn), and then have a cigarette, promising herself to quit "as soon as this is all over."
>
> Before that daily commute, both her ailing mom, Annie, and her husband, Bob, were living at her home. It was summer vacation. While her peers were languishing on the beaches of Hawaii or dancing the night away on a Princess Cruise, Vicki was playing nurse-referee to mom and husband. As an outgrowth of the horrible illness from which she was suffering, her mother got the mistaken idea that her immobile son-in-law was a threat. This woman, who only months before was a sweet, unselfish, quiet, charitable person was now stalking Bob's bedroom. Like in some

kind of bizarre spy movie, Vicki would be startled to discover her mother lurking behind a door or at the foot of his bed. Vicki worried that her tiny mother would do her helpless husband some harm, so she took her turn standing guard, keeping vigil till dawn, when the nurse showed up.

Soon Annie took a turn for the worse and needed full-time care. During the stressful week before she could set her mom up in a facility, Vicki asked her adult stepdaughter to take Bob for a little while. After just one week of caregiving, the daughter realized what a saint Vicki had been for the last year. After much discussion, they decided it was best to put Bob in a nursing home as well. Can you imagine Vicki's heartbreak? This is a selfless and devoted wife who kept putting off the inevitable. She had wanted to protect Bob from feeling abandoned. His faithful daughter was no less loving, but she had the courage to convince Vicki that it was time.

Right after Bob got settled into his nursing home, her mother died. Vicki and her two sisters were with her.

These are the sad and hideous situations we all want to avoid. But what choice have we? To temporarily douse it with alcohol? To sleep it away? Tempting. But eventually we come back to it. That's where the courage kicks in.

Vicki organized her mom's funeral services, which took place in her backyard, grieved with her sisters, and soon went back to teaching. Every day it took courage to get up, give as much as she could to her precious little first graders, check on her convalescing father, pay a visit to her husband, and come home burdened with guilt because he wasn't in his own home. This regimen lasted only for a short time, as her dad started to heal; but Bob seemed to be going downhill, and Vicki wanted to bring him home to die.

In order to do that she had to convert the dining room into a hospital room. She called a home-care agency and was able to get help in the form of a Fijian nurse named Asinate. She was a godsend. Asinate provided not only twenty-four-hour health care for Bob but became the one person who truly knew what Vicki was going through. And believe it or not, they laughed a lot. It was Vicki's relief. I think her tears were tired of flowing, so laughter became her medicine. The two of them have become giggling girlfriends, sharing the joys and sorrows of the life handed to them.

Bob remained in Vicki's dining room, deteriorating, for another year. When he passed, Vicki called upon her close friends to help her through her grief. We have been in awe of her courage and how she could always find something to giggle about—even in the most serious situations.

Vicki's sense of humor has been the sustaining quotient in this devastating situation. She has the gift. I think it comes from honest humility and a deep need to protect others from feeling sad. Her humorous way of looking at things is a direct route to her courage.

~

Nancy's fifty-three-year-old husband let his urologist tell her about his cancer diagnosis.

ALL YOU HEARD WAS THE C WORD

It was one of those moments you will always remember every detail of. The doctor put on his best poker face and said, "The bad news is that your husband has prostate cancer; the good news is that we caught it early." All you heard was the C word reverberating in your brain, which raced ahead with the first big question: Is he going to die? Somehow you never thought a moment like this would come so soon, at least not for you. That word will have so much power over you for the next decade of your life. It will be harder than you could imagine. It will profoundly affect your ability to have a biological child. It will affect your self-esteem. In retrospect, the whole experience was a tragicomedy—the comic parts getting you through the experience, the tragic moments inescapable. The visits to the emergency room after midnight, holding his hand as he gets his penis recatheterized after a blockage. The time the sex therapist shows you how to do penile injections and tells you to look at them as foreplay. You respond, "Maybe for the Marquis de Sade this was foreplay, but I'm not gettin' it!" The many moments you silently ached for him, knowing that for a man it's all about performance, and understanding that nothing you can say will make him feel better. Any major illness can be devastating and life altering for a spouse. Hopefully, you will get through it as we did. It gave my life a bittersweet quality: We conquered it, but it took something from us as well.

ACTIVITY: Recognize It

Is there someone in your life who's trying to handle tough times? Write this person a note clearly acknowledging how you see their courage. Doing so will actually boost the courage already there. If anybody needs to be recognized for their strength, it's this person. Don't put it off. Do it right now.

Is it you? Are you the one making it through tough times? Write the note anyway. Pretend you're writing it to someone else and give her kudos for the hard work she's doing making it through each day. Be specific about what it is she does.

Sadness Is Healthy

Have you noticed that laughter cannot be endured for longer than a few minutes at a time? In the best of situations we have a few outrageous moments of joyful releasing, then another and still another until our bodies are exhausted. It's the same with the emotion of sadness, and even with deep mourning. The strong feelings and the tears come in waves; then we get a little break before it starts up again. No one cries forever. Just like joyful laughter, crying is a healthy and essential emotional discharge. We get ourselves in trouble when we try to ignore these feelings or push them away. Fear and avoidance of feeling sad only exacerbate the situation and cause more stress and anxiety. The next time you feel sadness coming on, try something new: Flow with it. Let it out, let yourself cry. Take a crying walk or a bath and release the sorrow. With middle age comes sadness. This is a fact of life. The cycle is proceeding all around us, and death is part of that continuum. Good friends, family members, pets, and icons will all go the way of nature. And with their passing comes grief. Learn right now to let loose the tears and go with the feeling. It will serve you well as the years go on.

~

A sorrowful but common occurrence for most people in midlife is the loss of a pet. It's a fact we must all face—we outlive our pets. Common or not, it can be every bit as devastating as the loss of any other family member. Eva, forty-five, shares her story, with the hope that you will either relate to her loss or be more prepared when it happens to you.

TWENTY-FOUR HOURS WITHOUT SPENCER

I'm forty-five, single, and my son just died. Not my biological son. No. I haven't had one of those. This life didn't give me that. I never found the time, the man, or the wherewithal to have a child of my own. Yet I just lost my son. My boy. My pup. His name was Spencer. I'm finishing my first twenty-four hours without him. It's so painful. He was spunky, he was smart, and he was the only unconditional love I've ever experienced. He died while I was away on business. He had a blood disorder. I couldn't have known.

Waking this morning from the sleep I didn't have, I carried the feeling of drowning. Drowning in the sadness of his beautiful essence not around anymore. That little tan boy of mine didn't jump on the bed, didn't bring "Mr. Reddy"—his half-football, half-hippopotamus chew toy—up to drop on my head, didn't run to the door to let me know it was time for a pee. Silence was all I heard.

I got up to have coffee, but one sip was all I could swallow. Spencer liked to join me while I drank. Today, drinking was too painful. So I went back to bed. I shut my eyes and made it go away, but his cute little face kept appearing. I opened my eyes again, shut them. Where to go in my brain? There was nowhere. Nothing. I cried. Deep tears. It was only seven-thirty. I got up, I walked around, I looked at the places he always sat. I tried to eat a peanut butter and jelly sandwich. There isn't anywhere to go when what was such a huge part of your life leaves the earth.

He's my angel now; how I wish I could visit him in heaven. I wish I could talk to God and ask him if Spence could come back. Just for a moment, so I could say good-bye. But that wish would not be granted, for he was supposed to leave the earth plane while I was away so I couldn't see him suffer in his illness. I was to remember him in his joy. With his loving eyes looking at his mom with great, powerful glee. Minutes turned into hours yet I can't recall what I did, thought, or felt five minutes ago. I have to go to the philosophical place in order to keep from falling into a heap on the floor.

He's my angel now. As those that leave us always are. It's dinnertime and I'm not hungry. I can't eat. But I can remember my child, my Spencer . . . with grace, with appreciation, and with the knowledge that he was loved as much as he could be. Tomorrow's a new day, and maybe it will bring the slow healing of my heart. And maybe in time I'll be able to think of him without breaking down. I'm forty-five, single, and just lost my son. I loved you, Spencer; I always will, and the light of your spirit will shine around me and all the people you touched. Maybe that will give me healing tonight. Maybe.

The courageous Suzy, fifty-four, writes the following passage. It's included not to frighten or worry you but because we feel it's necessary to let you in on one woman's passage of losing her best friend. Some of us have already experienced this poignant journey; others are dreading it. Reading someone else's chronicle lets us know what to expect when our time comes and gets us in touch with that community of brave people who have suffered the loss of a soul sister.

Losing a close friend is unavoidable, and reading someone else's account helps us prepare for when it's our turn.

WHEN OUR BEST FRIEND DIES

This last year was a barn burner, and mostly I feel grateful I survived. My best friend died. Her name was Helen, and a smarter, more fun-loving, and dedicated human being did not exist. She backed up her stubborn stand against injustice with action and made a difference to the lives of her friends and to Native Americans in Montana and elsewhere. She recycled before anyone did, never used poisons in her home, and railed against those who did. She believed in the sanctity of the small businessperson and avoided all large corporate megastores with a passion. She spent most of her life in politics and was a lobbyist for Indian affairs. I spent a lot of time traveling with her, raising our children, shopping, working for candidates, eating, and arguing. She was positive and loved rock music; she attended Woodstock 2 and every other damn rock concert she could go to.

I miss her like crazy.

New Year's 1999 was when she began having what she called her "déjà vu" moments, when she would feel herself above the fray and looking down on everyone. Detached and alone, not in pain, yet frightened by this new sensation, she would check out, and I could see her figuratively stepping back—retreating. Retreating was not in Helen's makeup. She was a charger—an informed, thoughtful, well-prepared charger.

On January 10 I got a call saying she had had a biopsy, which had revealed a glioblastoma of some considerable size and was to be operated on immediately. I saw a picture of the thing, which she referred to as a Republican plot. On alternate occasions she called it Trent or Newt or by the name of any of a long list of political conservatives. The tumor was the size of a child's fist and squarely in the middle of her brain.

Tumors are numbered as to their virulence from one to four,

four being the fastest growing and most deadly variety. Helen had a number four.

Since Helen had to fight a royal battle, she chose what the doctors said was the only possible route. They hadn't met a more stubborn opponent than Helen or a more dedicated and determined fighter, and so they were encouraged to enter her name on a list of eighty participants over the United States who had agreed to the protocol.

I moved in with Helen on the January 14. She was beginning radiation therapy, and for a period of six weeks we went five days a week. Her doctor was an intelligent liberal, and I thought he was the perfect partner in our battle.

Her only desire the whole time was to be normal. Helen was a rock 'n' roll fan of long standing. In her attempt at normalcy she was determined to attend as many rock concerts as possible. That I have never liked to attend crowded, deafening, fan-crazed events didn't bother her at all. She was going, and if I wanted to tag along that would be fine. She bought tickets for Crosby, Stills, Nash, *and* Young, Bob Dylan, Leo Kottke, and Tina Turner. The radiation treatments were fitted in around the concerts, but they left her in a weakened state.

Many friends joined us, jamming themselves plus wine and food into our motel rooms. Helen laid like a diva on the king-size bed, surrounded by wine, women, and take-out containers. At the concert Helen rocked in her wheelchair and smiled the whole time.

Helen held great stock in Indian spiritualism. In February, Indian leaders from all over the country came to Missoula to honor Helen.

One wonderful day a group of Blackfeet drummers came to call. We had told Helen of their coming, but she must have forgotten, for when the leader came to her bedside and began to chant her eyes opened wide and she smiled broadly. I leaned in and said, "Some kind of fantasy, eh? A tall, good-looking Indian in your bedroom—and singing, too."

In Missoula there is an international choir festival. One afternoon we got a call from a friend who asked if the Botswana choir could come to sing for Helen. We couldn't say yes fast enough. A group of middle-aged women and one older man appeared, all dressed in comfortable, bright-colored summer clothes, and in they all trooped. They all lay hands on Helen and prayed mightily, and at a signal from the man they commenced singing. Helen gazed at them and closed her eyes, and a smile crossed her lips. She said nothing but held tightly to the man's hand, opening her eyes only when they were finished. They sang old spirituals and Botswanan folk ballads, and they sang straight from their hearts. They kissed her, then returned to the backyard.

One of the issues we dealt with was the approaching marriage of Helen's daughter. It was to be in late August, but Helen was nearing the end of her life in mid-July. In retrospect I think the wedding date should have been changed to include Helen. She didn't want that because she believed she would make it to the wedding. When is it wise to address the obvious? When is it time to say, "Put your house in order?" One wants to be positive and promote well-being, but when it became obvious that Helen's time was short, none of us, including her daughters and her doctor, were able to speak the truth. We tried, but our efforts were met with a shake of her head. Denial was her desire, and we complied. She couldn't support the idea of not being around, and to the end we comforted her and encouraged her, knowing that she would soon be gone.

The day came when she could no longer take part in the protocol. Her health could no longer support the extraordinarily strong medications. That was a hard day, because she knew that without them it was a hopeless cause. At that time she kind of checked out. She still talked and sometimes would laugh at some foolishness. I drew closer and would often lie down beside her and hold her hand and sing any song that came to mind. We would fall asleep sometimes, not knowing what time of day it was.

I grew to love Helen's daughters more than ever and was astounded at their bravery. But at the moment of death, at Helen's last breath, I turned to her younger daughter and said, "She's gone." The young woman bolted from the room and ran to the garden crying out for her mother. Her pain was too private to share. No matter how prepared you are for your mother's death, it is a shock of such strength and power that no one can predict how you will act. In fact, she went home and cut off her beautiful, long hair.

What followed was so utterly personal and unique that I am shy about relating it. We bathed Helen and dressed her in the dress she would have worn to the wedding. Then we wrapped her in a homemade "star quilt" that had been given to her by an Indian artist. Within the folds of the quilt we tucked totems and pictures and flowers. And then we let her lie overnight in her room while we spent time with friends in the garden and sometimes in her room, talking and singing and remembering Helen. The undertaker was to arrive at nine A.M. I told the girls to stay away during that time so that their last memory of their mother would be in the quilt.

I learned more about myself taking care of Helen than I did about anything else. I'm glad I made that journey with Helen, and I hope I can have the same courage when my time comes.

Today I went to Fred Meyer's drugstore intending to buy some dishwashing detergent. I looked for the "green" variety and couldn't locate it in the housecleaning section but finally found it in the natural-foods aisle. I became Helen then and suggested to the folks at Fred Meyer they put the environmentally healthful products with the other, more poisonous, cleaners so that folks could have a choice and not have to go looking for them. They agreed and said they would look into it. In so many ways Helen guides me still, and I find myself seeing things through her eyes.

How do you come back from that experience? Here are Suzy's thoughts.

There is no one road, and time does have a way of mitigating the pain, but each of us has in us the remnants of our friends' lives.

> Lives whose imprint is everlasting and unforgettable can be a great source of joy and strength. I think when you miss those qualities you loved in a friend, they remind you that you still need that humor or compassion. You won't find that communion in yourself, only in others. Listen to your inner voice and adapt to this change. The best way to mourn your friend is to develop the relationships you have and try to be open to new friendships. That said, I find myself in a puddle of depression despite having met and reacquainted myself with some very terrific women. So I bought some Charlie Parker CDs and comfort myself knowing I am beginning rehearsals tomorrow on a grand comedy. Activity is the answer. Selfishness can take over when you are in a funk. But getting out of yourself can be a good exit ramp off the autobahn of blahs.

Our Own Mortality

For many of us, watching our parents age and die and coping with their illnesses is our first close experience with the process of dying. The experience often profoundly affects us, as it did Nancy when her dear father-in-law was dying. Here's a short piece on death taken from her daily journal:

> I love my father-in-law. To me he is the sweetest curmudgeon who ever lived. We have this love affair, a kind of unspoken agreement that we will show only our best side to each other. Not everyone gets this side of him—or of me. I have watched his decline over this last year knowing I have precious little time left of this unique relationship.
>
> As I trudge down the hall of the critical-care unit I brace myself for what's to come. How will he look? I steal a glimpse into each open door on my way to his room. Every room is filled with people who look dead, only the machines are keeping them alive. "I don't want to die that way" is the thought that fills my head as much as sympathy for the dying. "That way" means helpless, shriveled up, unable to walk, talk, eat, think, pee, or

defecate. A perverse version of an infant, minus the newborn charm. I contemplate this as a future and shudder.

I walk into his room. Now it is someone I know and love that I see "like that" in front of me. "Why does it have to happen like this, Jack?" I take his hand in mine. Through a morphine haze a dreamy look comes over his face, and I can only hope he feels like an infant again.

I would like to wrap this dying thing up differently, all nice and neat, in a little package. "What am I supposed to learn from this, Jack?"

For that, there are no answers.

Things Are Always Changing

The hard stuff life brings us in middle age isn't all about death, but in one way or another we have to learn how to let go of "how it was" and get a grip about "how it is." Take the midlife woman and her midlife body. Things are changing. Things hurt, things don't stretch back, things are drying up. Oh, and that's not even the bad news. How we take care of ourselves is of utmost importance to our personal happiness in the future. Dr. Ricki Pollycove, a fifty-year-old San Francisco–based gynecologist, has some thoughts on the effort and commitment it takes to stay healthy.

OUR MIDLIFE BODIES

I think the misconception that you can have a better experience than your mother did as she aged—that is, making no personal effort and leaving all the work to the scientists and pharmaceutical companies—is incorrect. Women must come to the realization that getting older requires real effort and some financial commitment. The cheapest and easiest thing is to die early.

When a forty-five-year-old woman comes into my practice and she's still feeling spry, perky, and touchable, it shocks her to hear that she is already in her second half. The ones in denial will say, "The second half of what?" Becoming conscious is the very first step. We have to face the fact that we're already in middle of our life and must do something now to ensure a healthy future.

Life gives us the gift of resilience up to about the age of thirty-five. When you were younger you could abuse yourself—drink too much, stay out too late, experiment with drugs and sex—and still function, function, function. Many women now in their fifties were, in their thirties, a part of a high-performance group—they were smoking this and that, pushing themselves hard, and playing around with sleep deprivation. They burned themselves almost to the very limit of the wick. Women have to put in a concerted effort, do the hard work to stay healthy for the sake of their happiness in their future. Whether it's going to the gym regularly, keeping up a healthy, low-fat, high-fiber diet, scheduling regular check-ups, considering HRT, or eliminating the drugs or alcohol that may be slowing us down, if we want to be around to enjoy the gift of the second half, we have to get off our tushes and become proactive. We are the privileged ones—we have awareness. And we must act upon it.

Is It Hot?

The average hot flash lasts about three minutes. In about the time it takes for your hair conditioner to soothe your split ends, the blood lava slowly works its way throughout your body like the fiery coil of a heating element, until it accumulates in your head, frying off what memory cells you had left. And then it's over. Till next time.

Ah, but we're lucky. We live in a world full of baby-boomin' hot mamas. These days it's as common to see a woman with her face on fire as it is to see her pimply daughter on a cell phone. Technically, it's the mother who's the real "hottie."

No amount of yams will bring back the elasticity in our uterine walls, but at least we're all drying up, hanging loosely, and hot-flashing together. With that in mind, one might also assume it prudent to invest in K-Y Jelly stock. And how many of us are wishing we had started doing our Kegels a long time ago? No more trampoline for you, young lady . . . er . . . midlife lady.

As our body parts begin the drying-up process—that's eggs, eyes, skin, and vaginas—we need products. We also need to be educated about those products. Ask your doctor what new techniques, drugs, and natural options are on the market these days. Because of the sheer amount of middle-aged women in the consumer marketplace, pharmaceutical companies are working overtime to please and ease the poor little dry boomer. And products like Change-O-Life and Hot Flashex are among the many wild-yam items sitting on the health-food-store shelves for you to try. Remember the eighties group Dire Straits? I want my—I want my—I want my HRT.

There are crazy women everywhere. They're doing our hair, teaching our children, making our food, even representing us in Congress! They haven't yet done anything destructive enough to warrant institutionalization, but don't mess with them . . . they're on the brink. Their estrogen level is out of balance.

This imbalance can happen several times in a woman's life, from prepubescent hormonal swirls to PMS to postpartum depression; but nothing compares to menopause. And perimenopause can go on for many years before any true loss of the menstrual cycle. It's a no-man's-land—and no man should come near us when we're in a hormonal snit.

Questions about whether or not to use hormone replacement therapy are on the minds of most middle-aged women—and on their doctors' minds as well.

Marilyn talks about the moment she realized she was being pulled down by the hormonal undertow and what she found helpful.

WHEN IT'S MORE THAN PMS

At first I thought it was PMS. Well, a bigger, more evil kind of PMS. Some days it seemed like I could feel a surge of chemicals whooshing through my body, and then I'd be crying because a leaf fell from a tree and it was so poignant I couldn't bear it. I told my husband, "Look, we're gonna fight . . . *you* pick the topic." My ten-year-old daughter bringing me a handful of picked flowers would produce tears, but a minute later, I'd rage because she'd gotten them from the neighbor's yard.

One hot, wet sleepless night I got up and turned on the TV. The PBS station was showing a compelling documentary about the difficulties blacks faced in leaving Mississippi to go to Chicago in the 1950s. While watching all these scenes of hatred and poverty, I once again began to cry. For the next few days, whenever I would think about it, I would cry. I was feeling guilty simply because I was Italian. And extremely sad. My daughter came home from school angry because she had so much homework to do and I lit into her: "Homework! Is that all you've got to worry about? Think of the poor blacks in Mississippi!" I went through the whole documentary with her. I even had her crying. I was clearly over the edge.

I talked to my doctor about it, and he figured I was quite ready for hormone replacement therapy—right away. We tried Premphase, and after a month I felt like a big, heavy weight had been lifted off my shoulders. I was my regular old self. I was happy, thinking clearly, philosophical, humorous, and responsible. No heat, no tears. What a joy.

That was three years ago. Now I don't know what to do. As the controversy about HRT's side effects swells, so does my head. I stopped my HRT regimen for a month, but I couldn't stand the old, grouchy, hot me. Not everyone will feel it's the right therapy, but my recommendation is to seek help if you feel any of the symptoms I described.

Every woman should talk to her doctor about whether HRT is right for her. Benefits include reduced risks of osteoporosis, colon cancer, and Alzheimer's disease. Negatives include elevated risks for breast and ovarian cancer. Your doctor will help you decide which is best for your own special needs.

~

With age come many dysfunctions of certain body parts. This is a hard one for all of us. From ovarian cysts to poor eyesight to incontinence to arthritis, the list grows a little longer each year. JoAnne, forty-seven, talks about losing one of the good old standbys—her uterus.

HELP! MY UTERUS FELL AND I CAN'T GET IT BACK UP THERE BY MYSELF!

On my fortieth birthday my husband was so kind to throw a surprise party. Of course it included "humorous" gifts and a lot of information from my "older and wiser" friends about what to expect of my body now that it was forty.

The one gift that has come back to haunt me was a "thoughtful" gift from Sue: a bra generously sized 36 Long. The cups, resembling parfait cups, boasted the message "Help, fallen, can't get up!" Everyone laughed, advising me that I might as well go on vacation down south, as my body will with or without my permission. It's all fun and games when you're turning forty.

Two years later I was in an extremely energetic cleaning mode that involved moving the furniture to vacuum. I was pushing and pulling when I felt a very uncomfortable pressure, as if someting was protruding between my legs. I immediately and very cautiously made my way to the bathroom to investigate. Then I called my doctor. The nurse wanted the reason for my phone call. I paused for a moment and then said, "One of two things have happened: Either I just became a man or my uterus just fell out." I was told to come right into the office.

Upon examination, the doctor confirmed that I was still a woman and that indeed my uterus had made a most unwelcome appearance. She tried different pessaries to push my uterus back up and hold it in place. Every time she would insert a pessery, she would ask me to stand, and—surprise!—my uterus would reappear. After several long minutes of playing peekaboo with my body parts, she made a decision to remove the little bugger. The good news: Since the uterus was visible, they would be able to remove it vaginally. The bad news: People would be digging around my opening.

There was no time to fear or mourn the pending loss of my uterus, as the surgery was scheduled for first thing the following morning. I came to the realization en route to the hospital that, all things considered, I was actually ready to part with my baby-holder. I was fortunate to have two wonderful children, and I was not planning to have more.

The surgery went well, though it took a little longer than expected. My doctor discovered that my uterus had been kind enough to bring some friends with it. My ovaries, my bladder, and my vagina also dropped down to say hello. She reattached the little friends and—as a bonus—took an extra stitch to "Miss Vagina." (Guess who benefited from that one?)

It has been three years since that adventure, and I am thrilled to say that everything is great! I actually celebrated the loss of my uterus and received the gift of freedom. I no longer need to schedule vacations around my period, no longer need to worry about birth control, and sex is definitely more enjoyable without the worry of pregnancy.

I just celebrated my forty-seventh birthday, and it was no surprise to see that, yes, in the last seven years the boobs and butt did go on vacation without me. But hey, that's okay—that's what underwire and control top are all about. Only five more till I'm fifty. Do I dare ask my "older and wiser" friends what to expect?

Our Midlife Minds

Whether it's the all-too-common lost-keys syndrome, no clue where you left your car in which parking lot, or having trouble calling up the name of your best friend during a crucial introduction, we all have times when our memory goes haywire. Though many herbal companies claim that *ginkgo biloba* extractions will restore it, nothing really helps when you're in a pinch. Marilyn believes that laughing about the sorry side of aging is the only way to cope.

FORGET ABOUT IT

Forgetfulness has become a way of life for me. I am one with my slowness. In fact, I crack myself up. Take the time I went to the wrong high school reunion, where, because I'm so used to forgetting who people are, I had no clue I was in the wrong place.

It was my thirtieth high school reunion. I wasn't planning to attend, so I threw the invitation out. At the last minute my old girlfriends persuaded me to go, and when I asked where it was being held they said, "Oh, you know, at the old Round Barn," adding that a hotel had been built back where we used to park and make out with our boyfriends. However, my old boyfriends must have taken me to a different place, where a different hotel had been built, and, against all odds, there was a different high school reunion going on that exact weekend in November.

I had flown in from Cincinnati that night and was running a little late. Still not sure I had the right place, I went to the desk and asked if this was where the reunion was being held. The desk clerk pointed me to the second floor. The cocktail hour was still on so, I grabbed a glass of Chardonnay and proceeded to mingle.

So there I was smiling and nodding like a fool at people I don't even know. The thing is, they recognized me from television, so their brains said, "Familiar face equals classmate," and they gave a hearty "Hi!" as though I was their long-lost friend. There was nothing left for me to do but give them back an equally enthusiastic greeting. I was desperately searching for my girlfriends when I asked a group of overly dressed women if they had seen my friend Vicki. I guess the odds of someone named Vicki being at any given class reunion were also high, because they said she was over at the bar.

Lost and meandering, I made my way to the back of the room, where on the walls there were black-and-white blown-up photos of their good ol' years. That's when it finally hit me: Who were these people?

I grabbed a passing waiter and said, "Excuse me, is this Montgomery High, class if '65?" With a wide grin, he replied, "No, ma'am, this is Cloverdale, class of '75!" After I took in some air, we both started to laugh. I said, "No wonder they look so much younger than me. Here I was thinking, 'Hey, I'm not the only one here who's had a little work done!' "

Now, I can't imagine my memory getting any worse than it is, but at least I can still remember the story. When I've lost the capacity to tell somebody what an idiot I am and laugh about it, shoot me.

And Marsha, fifty-one, knows what it feels like to draw a blank:

WHAT'S HIS NAME?

I was telling my teenage daughter about a very funny episode of *Frasier* she'd missed the night before. I began by saying "So the two of them go to a basketball game—Niles and . . . Niles and . . . um, you know, his brother. Kelsey Grammer." She had that look in her eyes, the way they all looked at Captain Queeg in *The Caine Mutiny* when they realized he was nuts. She said, "His name is Frasier, Mom—just like the show. You just said you were watching *Frasier*. That's why it's called *Frasier*." Until she said that I had no idea what his name was on the show. On the show called *Frasier*.

Midlife Independence

Many women in midlife—by choice or not—live alone. For many independent women, this is a point of pride. For others, it seems like the dream of being married and having kids is fading. And for the newly divorced woman, living alone may be the first independent act she's undertaken. Life gives us challenges, and life gives us disappointments. How we choose to handle them will determine the outcome of the second half of our life.

Though the "single woman" stigma that once sat heavily on our mothers' shoulders no longer exists, and neighbors, having much bigger fish to gossip about, have let go of the old "divorcée next door" threat, the hardship of living alone continues to be its own beast.

Nancy talks about having to be alone in the winter without her husband.

CINDERELLA AND THE SPACE HEATER

I remember thinking, "How did it come to this?" Stranded in a house so cold I could see my breath, I was sopping wet from snow, sweat, and tears, with my golden retriever licking the mascara running down my face. I was alone, frustrated, and unable to get my car—which was supposed to take me to my seventy-hour-a-week job, the only solid thing I thought I had—out of six feet of snow.

I picked up the phone to call my estranged husband at his warm apartment, and angry words spewed out. "It's all your fault, goddamn it! I'm snowbound, there's no heat, I can't get to work—and you can't decide if you want to be married anymore! goddamn you!" I screamed as I slammed down the phone. Of course it was all his fault.

I was in disbelief. A few years before, we'd been the couple on top of the wedding cake, and this old farmhouse in its shabby state of disrepair had seemed romantic. That was before our marriage became like that experiment of the early nineties, "the commuting two-career couple." Sometimes our dreams materialize, then disintegrate, and we find ourselves alone in a fairy tale gone bad.

I clearly recall the epiphany I had that day. It was one of those moments in which you remember every detail. Joni Mitchell was singing about wanting to skate away on a river in the background.

I called the marriage counselor crying my heart out, asking, "What am going to do?" She listened to my emotional rantings and softly responded, "First, get a space heater."

Then it hit me. All along I'd thought I was so independent, so capable, so together, but I didn't even have the basic skills to keep myself warm. Like a latter-day Scarlet O'Hara, I vowed that I would never be cold again, and to this day, at forty-seven, I haven't been—except by choice.

Fearless Homecoming

If you happen to live in a town other than where your parents live, visiting them during the holidays or on any other occasion can have an effect on your spirit. One preparation we almost never do is ready ourselves for the actual reunion—and all that this event brings up within our unsuspecting psyche. All too often we pack unrealistic expectations along with our holiday outfits. We have put together a guideline for adults when they go home for a visit.

Here's Marilyn's take:

I am an adult woman. I'm vital, creative, and ageless—until I go back to my mother's house for the holidays. It's the one time I'm forced to look in the mirror and see another reality.

No matter what year—or century—it happens to be, when I walk up the steps to that front door I'm fifteen and I've just come home from "tooling town" with some junior boy, and my mom thinks I've been at the library. The spell is broken when my mother greets me. Who is that elderly woman?

Her house isn't as spotless as it used to be. Her chair is too close to the television. She struggles to walk.

And so I take my place in the rank and file of our family. I'm not a carefree adolescent fibbing about my whereabouts. I'm an adult woman . . . the oldest of three, with four adult children of my own and a worn-out mother.

When did the shift happen? When did my mother become my grandmother? There is no rite of passage ceremony for this changing of the guard. No one crowned me Miss Middle Age. But when I really think about it, it's been seeping into my consciousness little by little. My eyesight, my memory, my sagging elbows—some of Mother Nature's little hints. And denial doesn't work out so well when you go back home.

As I walk into the restaurant I stand there a minute and search for my crazy friends, only to be seated at a table with some old ladies. Apparently plastic surgery isn't a priority back home. Instead of sex and AquaNet, we talk about our aches and pains, our latest diagnosis, and our favorite drugs. Everyone has a story of some kind of loss. There are only two Beatles left. It doesn't take long before I'm feeling grateful I still have my mother. And this other magical thing begins to happen: I see that I'm not alone. They share my resistance, my fears, my gratitude, my gray roots. The impetuous teens are now clever, intuitive, grown women. We reminisce over aged wine, and the laughter—along with endorphins—begins to wash away the anxiety. Our laugh lines are well earned and necessary.

I am reminded that without my support system I'm overwhelmed and lost. Thank God for old girlfriends!

Nancy adds this vital message:

The amazing thing about going home for a visit is that while we have changed and grown (as have our parents), we somehow forget that we can't change the addictions, bad habits, or annoyances of our family members. Even though we weren't able to make Dad stop drinking those eighteen years we lived at home, most of us think that somehow we can do it now. Wrong! You must remember that even though you may be educated, enlightened, and therapized, your parents haven't been. So save yourself the energy and heartache and let go!

Here's a little warning, however—you have to let go and try not to judge them, but don't expect them to let go and not judge you. Remember, you are the one who is educated, enlightened, and therapized, not them. So when Mom still gripes about why you don't do things her way, why you can't be the kind of housewife she was, why you haven't produced grandchildren yet, or any number of things that irritate her, grin and bear it.

The most important realization of all may be that you can love your parents for who they are and who they are not. To love them fearlessly and not try to change them. Try that famous little serenity prayer: "God grant me the serenity to accept the things I cannot change, the courage to change the things I can, and the wisdom to know the difference."

Before going home, whether it's during the holidays or for a simple summer visit, do a little mental preparation and you can turn it into a rich and satisfying event. These five steps will help you to stay STRONG.

S—Support system. Make sure you have a good support system in place—whether it's with your siblings, your adult kids, your mate, your cousins, or your old friends. Take some time to be alone with them so you can reveal your true feelings and hear theirs.

T—Talk, tolerate, treasure, trust. You might see your family only occasionally. Why waste that precious time trying to change someone else or convince them you are "right"? In the big picture—what does it really matter? Talk lovingly. Tolerate the differences. Treasure these moments—they will be gone. Trust that family love will prevail.

R—Respect. Respect your parents for who they are. Respect their rules—no matter how petty or antiquated they seem. Respect your siblings. Their life is their business. Your visit is temporary.

O—Own up to who you are. Acceptance is the key. The line between who you were and who you are can get blurred when you visit home. Take stock in the adult you. Handle the annoyances like an adult.

N—Nonjudgment. Remind yourself not to judge your parents, and how they chose to parent you through the years. They raised you in the best way they were capable of at the time. Nonjudgment applies to not judging yourself as well. You did the best you could at being their child. Look to the future, don't judge the past.

G—Gratitude. If you think about it, there are many things to be grateful for. Make a list before you leave and look at it once in a while during your visit.

Am I Invisible?

Inevitably, the sweet bloom of youth fades—but acceptance of this doesn't always come easily. It's very difficult to admit your disappointment with what life has given you. As the window of opportunity to have kids, find a mate, or become a rock star gets smaller, we must find our way to fulfillment, and we must keep those precious friendships close at hand. Fifty-two-year-old Jan talks about her struggle.

> As a child, I was the "smart one" and my sister the "pretty one." In truth, she was just as smart and got big breasts to boot. (Try to tell me that life is fair!) In any case, the tags stuck. Then as a freshman in college, I got a big surprise: Boys started coming around telling me I was beautiful. Thanks to the wonders of hormones and my mama's genes, I had somehow turned pretty! It was a miracle, but one I readily accepted. After all, this stuff was classic Cinderella.
>
> I assumed that my magical transformation was permanent. I became used to turning men's heads when I walked into a room, to getting instant attention whenever I chose to join a party conversation. Twenty-five years passed, and the ball went on. I was older, had fatter thighs, looser skin, and my breasts weren't quite so perky, but I was still dancing.
>
> Then one day, I started talking to a man standing near me. I wasn't even flirting, but I got very little response. I tried again and realized that this man was looking right through me, all his attention on the younger women in the room. He was so uninterested in me that I might as well have been invisible. It was

then that I got it. Midnight had struck, and I had just turned back into a kitchen drudge. It was a terrible blow.

Though I didn't have much to say for the rest of the party, I had plenty to think about. I had just been tossed out of the exciting world of sexuality and romance, a world that had formed my identity all my adult life. The ball was over, and I was stuck with the ugly mess of the morning after. Suddenly, I didn't know how to be, what I wanted to be, even what I could be.

I went out and bought a house all by myself and furnished it like a *Victoria* magazine cover shot. No need to bother with earthy masculine touches when the only male in the house is the dog. He doesn't mind pink at all.

It's different, I grant you, but I am unapologetic. Just because men and most of society dismiss me because I'm no longer a young hot body doesn't mean I have to go along with it. I've slowed down, I've settled down, and it's a good thing. Now when I go to parties, I don't have to attract attention with my looks. My mind and personality are all I need. I not only have more to say, but a greater capacity to listen. There's no romance, but men and women like me better than ever. I like me better than ever.

I'm thrilled my hormones cranked up and made me what I am, and I thank God they died down and left me on my own to become something much more.

We all want to be noticed, we all want to be thought of as a worthwhile, contributing human being.

QUESTIONS

What things do you do to keep from being invisible?

Are they constructive or destructive?

Put your thoughts down here or in your journal, or brainstorm about this with your support group.

Little thrills can also come with being independent. After her divorce Garland got a little power surge.

THE SUMP PUMP

I had just moved into my house in June, but the rains flooded up through my basement floor and I had five inches—yes, five inches—of water sloshing around. I freaked out because the sump pump couldn't handle all the water and I was a woman alone. I called my architect dad from Virginia, who remembered how the sump pump was attached. He told me to get a garden hose, gaffer's tape, and a knife. I felt like I was a passenger on a small plane where the pilot had suddenly died and I had to bring the plane in for a landing. I cut and spliced and taped and, by crickey, I rigged up the pump to expel five inches of water from the entire basement in an hour. I am woman, hear me roar!

QUESTION

Who in your life has modeled that being alone is perfectly fine?

If your answer is "no one," then keep writing to learn how this fact has manifested itself in your way of thinking.

Independence or loneliness? That's a matter of attitude. You can be lonely even if you live with many people and several animals. We all feel a little lonely from time to time, but if you think you have chronic loneliness, it's time to talk to a professional. Talk to your family doctor, a licensed counselor, a religious leader, or your best friend and ask for help.

Forty-year-old Penny writes about her friend Kathryn's acceptance of her own independence and where it took her.

THERE'S A REASON FOR EVERYTHING

At forty-seven, Kathryn had stopped thinking she would get married. She'd had boyfriends, including a college relationship that had continued long after graduation, but she'd never found the "right" man. Recently, she'd moved home to Texas to be closer to her family. She loved her work and enjoyed spending time with her mom, her sisters, and her young niece and nephew. Even better, after years of roommates Kathryn had a sweet little apartment all her own, where nobody ate her cereal or stole her only pair of clean socks. Life was good.

Eventually she decided that she wasn't looking for someone to spend her life with. Dating was great, but she valued her independence and gradually decided that she was meant to be alone. So she was completely thrown for a loop when a mutual friend introduced her to a new man. They fell in love almost immediately and married the next year. Of course, we tease Kathryn relentlessly about how she was never, ever getting married, but when you see her with her husband it's obvious they were made for each other. They are a true couple; supportive and loving and glad for every minute they spend together. In fact, if you weren't so happy for them you could get sick with envy! They're such a twosome that now you can hardly imagine one without the other. I use Kathryn as an example to my unmarried friends all the time. Not only can you get married after forty, but there may be a perfect reason why you've waited that long.

Lost at Fifty

Sixty-year-old Tina thought she was cruising through midlife crisis free—until dealing with her aging parents put her into a "fifties funk" that she couldn't shake:

> It was not until my early fifties that I became lost. My once great looks were betraying me. I was no longer exercising, had had a

hysterectomy, and was looking as matronly as could be. My feet were happier in lower heels, and I started needing glasses to read. It was brutal. I envied the twenty-year-olds knowing full well their sleeveless dresses and their high, high heels would look silly on me.

I was also lost because my whole social life consisted of caring for my aging parents. They were both ninety and utterly unable to care for themselves. I did it out of love, obligation, and because there was no one else to do it. And even if a person takes on such a tremendous job out of love, the job itself wears you down. There was no more "me" in this equation.

I was stuck before the next stage, stalled between stations. I admit that sometimes it could be cozy and inert there, and I could have stayed in that stage reading easy novels, playing solitaire, watching old movies forever except for the fact that there was a niggling murmur of sadness underlying my life. There was sadness under everything like a subway, way, way underground but threatening to rip through with its force and speed, and then quiet down again.

I knew I was in trouble and had to make some changes. I had done mountain climbing to nineteen thousand feet in my forties and now had a new mountain to climb—*inside* me and it was tough, so tough. I flailed around eating ice cream and a brownie knowing the answer wasn't there but unable to know what to do next. The old answers weren't appropriate for this age but what was? *What was*?

Since I felt it was boring to bother my friends with all my problems, I concocted a way to reach them by shaping lovely stories, which I then gave them to read. Stories about love, aging, elderly parents, grandchildren, loss, and anger, and silly ones, too. The reaction was wonderful, and the reception to my stories led to working on a novel, which is a way for me to once again experience youth and folly and passion.

And, finally, I took the initiative and moved my aging parents to a home. This was so painful, but ultimately necessary. They raged against me. They felt betrayed by me as a substitute for the betrayal of their bodies and minds. When they refused to hear me, I had my husband tell them I could no longer take care of them—and I finally burst into tears, completely broken. I told my father I should not be giving up my life for them, that it was selfish of him. And he caved in. I divided their belongings and they took the best with them and I cleaned out their debris of sixty years of marriage, and had the place painted and sold. This began my freedom, as I no longer had to worry about them in the same hands-on way.

Little by little I began to do things for myself. I started with massages, haircuts, manicures, pedicures. It was strange and uncomfortable at first to be doting on myself, but I got used to it. I eventually went on trips. Creativity began to flow once more. My husband of twenty-seven years was wonderful as I pouted and kicked and experimented through my fifties. No longer dragging around a sense of being lost, I saw a little light at the very end of that long tunnel. Now, at sixty, I feel illuminated.

Today, it's the light of wisdom that seems to emanate from me. My feet are planted firmly in the next stage. I accept my aging self with pleasure. I know that to help the young is the answer. I am not threatened by them, but appreciate all that youth stands for and revel in the beauty they have, as well as all that we who are sixty have. If asked now how I feel about life, I can truly answer, "Never better."

The Empty Nest

Another way a woman in midlife can find herself alone again is when her children grow up and out. It's an extremely difficult hurdle to cross—the loss of your children. Yes, put that way it sounds so maudlin, but for some of us, when our babies grow up and leave home it is like a little death. It's certainly the death of our role as "Mom, the provider of dental appointments, phone messages, nutritious food, ironed shirts, toothpaste, and deodorant." Our job as "Mom, the watchdog"—not sleeping until they walk in the door at night, leaving the porch light on for them, and knowing their basic daily schedule—comes to a screeching halt. And so does "Mom, the busy and fulfilled person." Though we've been teasing for years that their room will now become the long-awaited sewing room, the anticipation of an empty house is a frightening day-dream. This style of becoming alone is quite an adjustment for most women.

Marilyn talks about her struggle with letting go.

MY BABY

I'm really over the edge. I've already said good-bye to two boys, and now my baby girl is a junior in high school, so I fear the worst is yet to come. I'm sure most of you will roll your eyes when you read this sappy stuff, but I must confess—my kids fill my heart. Even in the roughest of the teenage years—and I can "out-rough" most of you—I still want to soak up all the precious kid-essence I can before I'm truly abandoned. I know I need therapy; the question is: Do you?

Ten years ago when my oldest son was a senior in high school, he wore this black T-shirt with the words GOING, GOING written on the front; even bigger on the back was GONE. Let me tell you, the "going, going" part was far worse than anything. For me, that senior year became a litany of "lasts": the last back-to-school night, the last corsage to buy for the last dance, and, in my case, there was the relief of the last call from the principal.

Sometimes I'd see my boy napping on the couch on a warm Sunday afternoon and get jolted with memories of his toddler days, when he'd fall asleep on that same couch with his blankie. I'd just stand there longing to hold him again, knowing I could never do that . . . not like I used to. Throughout his senior year I'd try to get him to sit on my lap again . . . though I don't recommend doing that—they get really irritated with you. They swear, even.

Actually, fighting can help. As hard as that is, the kids usually do a mighty good job of getting you ready for their departure. Let me tell you, when you have to watch them make the same stupid mistakes you once made and snap at you for trying to prevent it, it really can grind on you. It's best that they do their little experimenting away from your sight and hearing. Kids are a little too open these days, at least in my case, and since I had no say in how many girls he dated at once, how many hearts he was hurting, or how many condoms he was using, and since it was nearly impossible to keep my mouth shut, it wasn't long before I could see the benefits of living apart. Yet it wasn't easy. I still miss him.

Now to face the last one out. It's a classic: My daughter is the baby of the family, and I'm pathetic when it comes to visualizing my life without her. I've got tears in my eyes as I write this. And she's still got two more years. Two short years. I've begun the process of making myself much more independent from her, but I secretly wish we could always live together, like those old twins in San Francisco. It's so much easier when they're evil.

My plan?

1. Therapy, therapy, therapy.
2. To trust that the sadness lasts for only so long.
3. I'll begin doing more things with my husband right now.
4. I'll get a new dog the day she goes. Is four too many?
5. Cry until it's over.
6. I'll get new drugs. Do they make a "letting go" drug yet?
7. I'll start something new—something time-consuming.
8. I'll give an empty-nest therapy party . . . only devastated moms can come.

And then there are those women who thought that by the time they were in their late forties they would be winding down from career and/or motherhood. Women who looked forward to living alone. To forty-nine-year-old Patty, there is no such animal as an empty nest.

DIVIDED

I'm a schoolteacher who was recently reminded that it was time to prepare for my retirement. Retirement? Already? Gee, I guess I should start my golf lessons. I am so far away from what I thought I'd be doing in my fifties. First of all, I have a four-year-old daughter who's in preschool. Between using my sick days to volunteer at her school in order to be a "good mother" and to fly out of state to take care of my aging mother in order to be a "good daughter," I see no time for a Caribbean cruise in the near—or far—future.

My daughter came to me quite late in life and, frankly, is my utmost joy. What she brings into my heart is what keeps me going when it's aching for my nearly blind, acutely arthritic mother. I guess it's sort of a balance God has given me, because otherwise I couldn't take it. I hate being so far away from my mom. I call and have to watch out for her from afar. All the while my nest gets filled up with *Good Night Moon* and ear infections and back-to-school night and correcting papers and church fund-raisers and extremely late microwaved dinners with a very tired husband. And none of it is a good enough excuse for not calling my mom today. Sometimes I can't take the guilt. Am I ready for retirement? You betcha. But who's going to pay for mom?

ACTIVITY: Gains and Losses

At every crossroads of your life there are things to be gained, and there are losses, as well. The following is a list of ten of the most common losses we might experience during our midlife.

Rearrange the list in order of importance to you, 1 being the most dramatic loss and 10 meaning no big deal.

___memory
___health
___elasticity
___close friends and family

___sexuality
___bladder control
___waistline
___uterus
___sanity
___children in the house

Look at your top three. What do they tell you about yourself? Is there anything you can do to help yourself regarding those top-three situations that you are not currently doing? For example, if health is high up on your list, do you do whatever is necessary to keep you healthy? If the friends-and-family category is number 1, are you free of any old anger or resentment? Are you showing them how much you truly appreciate them? If it's the empty nest that's worrying you, are you creating your support system for when the time comes? Are you looking into something new to occupy your time?

If you are worried about these things without actively doing something about them, then you are putting more concern into your losses than necessary. You cannot change what nature will eventually take away, but you can control the excess stewing over it. And don't forget the power of having a good old pal.

~

We did not touch on all the hardships that can come with middle age. That's a book unto itself. We mentioned some of the most common ones and shared other women's stories so you would not feel alone, and so that you'll be prepared for some of what's ahead. The next three chapters also deal with the preparation side of changing your life, and the last five chapters set you up to take action. But first, let's look at a few of the benefits of being in the middle of your life. In fact, there are many things about living past forty-five that bring us joy! And it's all in how you look at it. Take memory loss: It's good, because we can keep reading our favorite book over and over again and still wonder every time how it will end. But it's bad because we can't remember where we put the darn book.

THE GOOD STUFF

Five Solid Reasons Why It's Good to Be Old

1. **Experience.** You rock! Youth has nothing on you. Youth can't factor in your life experiences. The wide-eyed, smooth-skinned ones can't discern what is B.S. versus what is not quite the way you can. And they have a much harder time walking away from it. You don't have to put up with the power games people play, and you're a hard one to con these days.
2. **Perspective.** Youth does not yet know to trust in life's rhythm. You've lived long enough to understand that when there are bad times, good times will follow. Those in their twenties or even their thirties haven't encountered enough up and down cycles to know it's the natural way of the universe. When you're over forty you can get through those rough periods without fear that they'll never go away.
3. **Insight.** There's an acceptance we seem to gain only in later life—that it's not all about having fun and being happy. It's about courage and kindness and leaving this world a better place. We come to this understanding through experiencing our own losses.
4. **Self-Assurance.** We're not nearly as needy as we used to be. And without having to be on the constant prowl for a sex partner, we have the opportunity to explore who we really are and what we have to offer.
5. **Appreciation.** We've been through hardships, we've watched others struggle. We've seen how the rest of the world lives, and we can appreciate the little things.

As we mentioned, it's all in how you look at it. Here's one of fifty-year-old Bev epiphanies.

> Some days I feel trapped between a nice rock and a hard place. But thinking about it, it's not a bad situation to find oneself in!

I'm one of the "oldsters" among the kids I attend courses with at the junior college. But in my community oil-painting class, my fifty-year-old status puts me on the "junior attendance roster," while the majority of my classmates in that atelier are over fifty-five and on a separate attendance sheet!

It actually feels good to be neither here nor there with the age thing. Right now, I can both benefit from my still youthful exuberance and enjoy the reassurance of feeling a part of the "been there, done that, let's do it again" generation of seniors.

This transition from young to old will occupy a good chunk of my lifetime—why not enjoy being here?

What Real Women Think

We gathered a group of eight women aged forty-five to fifty-five to discuss what they thought the benefits of being middle-aged were. See if you can relate to any of the following observations.

- "I love that I'm no longer always wondering how I am doing."
- "Who I wanted to be with when I was twenty-five is very different from who I want to be with today, and it's so much more fulfilling. In those days, there was a little more in the success, money, and style category. Now what I value is integrity, intelligence, kindness, manners, and humor."
- "I just don't take myself so seriously—as though everything gone wrong is put into the disaster category—anymore. And after the true disaster of September 11, I'm ashamed of the heights to which I would take some of my mediocre daily problems. I can ride them out now with shrug of a shoulder."
- "When we were younger some of us were thought of as weird, flaky, and wild, and now they're beginning to call us eccentric! I love that."
- "I feel better than ever about myself. So what if the knee is hurting and these additional ten pounds are no longer extra but part

of! I like my age. All fifty years of it. The only thing is . . . I still get zits."

- "The best part? We still have a whole other part of our life ahead of us."
- "We can finally take a compliment!"
- "I am willing to be stupid. In my younger days, I was too insecure to reveal my ignorance—which was vast—so I faked it. I'm still pretty ignorant, but now I'm willing to say, 'I don't know about that, tell me about it.' It's the only way to learn, and it includes people rather than excludes them."
- "I seem to be having a sense of humor about everything now. Even if I don't get it."
- "The best advice I ever got was, 'Don't let turning fifty make you crazy—that is when you find your power.' And it's true. Our power takes many forms—like patience or silence—and now we have the insight to recognize it and use it."
- "We can put things into perspective much faster and make choices according to our priorities, not just because we can't say no."
- "We have much more confidence in our insight and instincts. Where I used to question if my instincts were just paranoid doubts, I now find that I'm right on most of the time."
- "I enjoy the quiet time. Now that my kids are no longer begging for my attention every other minute, I treasure reading and painting and gardening."
- "As we age do we become more noble. We think in terms of how to make the world a better place. And because we now have the wisdom, we become responsibly more liberal every year."
- "I know the friends I now have in my life will be my friends for life."
- "I'm just not so needy as I used to be. I don't need as much coddling or protecting or attention. I hope it stays that way."
- "I'm not tormented anymore. Not as intense. When I was young I was a tormented soul. Now I really am a happy person. What a relief."

Debunking Some of the Misconceptions

This group of real women also went on to separate some misunderstandings about the realities of aging:

Wrong: Women lose their sex appeal after forty.
Reality: Does the name Rene Russo mean anything to you?

Wrong: Once we retire, we'll finally have time for hobbies.
Reality: Very few people of the baby-boom generation plan to retire at all. Most of us have decided to simply switch jobs and embrace a new lifestyle. Hobbies and passions are to be enjoyed right now—and might be able to earn us a little money, as well.

Wrong: Once a woman reaches a certain age she must wear her hair short. (Ten more years and she must perm.)
Reality: Those rules were broken when Emmylou Harris turned fifty.

Wrong: If you're fifty and planning to apply for a job—forget about it.
Reality: Anita Roddick of The Body Shop started a hugely successful company in midlife. Frances Lear—simply the wife of a powerful man until she got divorced and found *her* power—started her own magazine, *Lear's*. And what about Senator Hillary Rodham Clinton—a powerful woman whose political career started after she turned fifty?

Wrong: By the time we reach our middle years, we should have "grown up" so we can "act our age."
Reality: Acting our age just might mean skipping down the street, laughing out loud in the movie theater, and continuing to wear barrettes in our hair (there isn't an age limit listed on the packaging for hair clips). It's all about freedom, baby!

Wrong: When you turn fifty you stop wearing see-through lingerie.
Reality: Unless you're dating some young stud, men of a certain age can't see that well anymore anyway, so what does it matter?

Wrong: By the time grandkids come, we are to be responsible, God-fearing adults.
Reality: Once the grandkids come along, it's best to hide the pot.

Wrong: All the good men are taken.
Reality: After living through some long-term relationships and perhaps even having gotten their hearts broken, good men grow into even better ones, learning more about being patient, supportive, and appreciative.

Wrong: Age brings with it the wisdom to accept the faults and annoying behaviors of others.
Reality: A jerk is a jerk is a jerk!

Some women see the good side of midlife in strange little places. Laura, fifty-one, is one of them.

THE SILVER LINING

One day I was leaning my face on my hand and I felt this bump against my finger, by my ear. I thought I'd developed a lump of considerable size since the last time I'd touched that part of my face, so I thought it must be a particularly devastating and fast-growing tumor; whatever it was, it had to be serious. Yet it disappeared when I removed my hand, and I instantly realized that it was loose skin. I had no idea it sagged to the point where I could push it into roll against my ear. I was aghast and wanted to do something about it immediately.

I'd also been thinking of returning to the dermatologist and once again getting a treatment for a troublesome brown spot on the side of my face, where the pigment keeps returning. I realized with mixed emotions that if I just had my face tucked, the brown spot would wind up behind my ear, saving me a trip to the dermatologist.

Well, I still haven't had that tuck, but I remember hoping that all the crumby little things about aging would have those silver linings.

Too bad so many people have a vision of a woman in midlife as being very old. Old lady kind of old. Ruth Buzzi on *Laugh-In* kind of old. Today's midlife woman—fifty and single—looks great! Did you know Norma Desmond in *Sunset Boulevard,* the pitiful has-been desperately praying for a comeback, is supposed to be fifty-five years old? Didn't anyone tell her that fifty-five is a great age? Where is Goldie Hawn when we need her? This next creative visualization is to help you dispel the "old lady" image.

Creative Visualization: The Muumuu

(NUMBER TWO ON CD)

Get into a comfortable position, either sitting in a chair, cross-legged on the floor, or lying down. Close your eyes. Begin to inhale through your nostrils and exhale through your mouth, gradually intensifying the deepness of your breath. With each inhalation, expand your stomach and chest, filling up your lungs with air, and with each exhalation, empty your breath from your chest and stomach until they feel "collapsed." Do this very slowly. Breathe in through your nose to the count of four, hold your breath to the count of seven, then slowly exhale from your mouth to the count of eight. With each new breath imagine yourself pulling in positive energy and everything you need, and with each exhalation feel yourself letting go of negativity and everything you don't need in your life. Do this several times.

See yourself standing on a secluded, beautiful, pristine, white sandy beach on a warm afternoon. Listen to the soothing sounds of the waves gently hitting the beach. No one is around for miles. You are wearing an old-fashioned muumuu. You've got a yellow plastic visor on your head, white socks and sensible sandals on your feet. You're laying out your towel, your sun umbrella, your handy beach chair, your romance novel, your cooler of sodas and a big basket.

Look at you: There you are with your big old muumuu and all your accoutrements. You look like a happy old woman ready to lounge comfortably. But you're not ready to lounge yet. You've still got a lot of energy, and the warm ocean water is calling you. You begin to take off your sandals, then your socks. No one is around, and no one will be coming for hours. You are wearing absolutely nothing under your muumuu.

You fling off your old muumuu and, completely naked, go into the water. It's warm and beautiful . . . and so are you. You swim and play. The longer you are in the water, the more healthy and energetic you feel. Play in the warm water for a while. You are having so much fun you wish you could share this feeling with someone else. But it's your time to be alone and pamper yourself. Now you're ready to go back to your spot on the beach. The sun feels glorious on your body. All is good. As you approach your towel, umbrella, and handy chair, you notice that your socks, sandals, and muumuu are missing. No matter.

You reach into your basket and pull out something else to wear. This time it's something more stylish, more hip, more fun. It tells the world who you really are! What is it you're putting on? You feel great! You are vibrant, energetic, and cute all rolled into one happy woman. You sit down and relax under your big umbrella. The sounds of the waves are so soothing. You reach into your basket again and pull out a journal and a beautiful pen. The first words you write are: *I am a beautiful, energetic, healthy, happy woman.* You like what you wrote so much that you write it again: *I am a beautiful, energetic, healthy, happy woman.* Keep writing it.

In a moment you are going to come back to the present, feeling relaxed and refreshed. Begin by taking three deep breaths. Notice the outside sounds. Start to wiggle your fingertips and your toes. Breathing regularly, open your eyes.

Share

Don't forget to process this visualization with your group or a friend or to write about it in a journal.

ACTIVITY: The Old Lady Party

Have a sleepover with as many girlfriends aged forty or older as you can muster up. Invite everyone to come dressed as an old woman. Have fun with it. Maybe send a pair of old white gloves or a hat along with the invitation. When your guests arrive have rock 'n' roll on the CD player and begin the fun. While everyone is dancing and partying, you've arranged it so that each guest gets a little time with a masseuse (there are people who need hours of practice in order to get their license and will do this for very little money), then a makeup artist (again, contact your local beauty school or get someone's teenage daughter to do it), and, last, a fashion consultant (sometimes a local dress shop will provide this service). Then take a good look and a lot of pictures of your captivating pals as they flaunt their "new" selves around. Later send them their "before" and "after" photos, reminding them how beautiful they really are.

~

Consciously or not, we react on some level to the hardest parts of aging. Whether to protect ourselves from sadness or to pretend we're still in our thirties in order to have one last fling, or baby, or face-lift, we all try to avoid the hard stuff. That's what a midlife *crisis* is. It's a reaction to fear. Fear of losing our youth, losing our "last chance" for happiness, losing our ego, our health, our dear friends. And it's a reaction to the suspicion that we might be missing out on the part of life we just dream about. When you look at what to expect and begin to prepare yourself for it, you give yourself inner strength. When you take a good look at all there is to being in the middle of your life, you will see all kinds of new possibilities. Then you can take the future by the horns and ride it—and bring some of your good buddies with you.

Chapter Three

Turning Point No. 3: Let Go of What's Not Working

YOUR MOTHER'S MIDLIFE: *Not all our mothers have lived the second half of their lives as unhappy, resentful, or sad women. However, for those of her generation who weren't blessed with an easygoing personality or a life free of bitterness, much of it was painful. Years ago, women didn't have therapy to help them determine their underlying resentments. Often the only confidantes our mother felt she could discuss her hurt and angry feelings with were her minister, a girlfriend, or her own mother. Typically the advice was either to forgive and forget or to ignore it. Some women turned to prayer to get through; others turned to Jim Beam. Some just went to their graves unhappy and unfulfilled.*

YOUR MIDLIFE: *When we perpetuate hurt feelings, hold on to bitterness, fear others' opinions, and serve with resentment we sabotage our chances for true happiness. After forty or so years it's likely you will see patterns of your own behavior that benefit your well-being and some that work against you. Instead of continuing on the same old course until you die, we're suggesting that you take inventory now and use this new awareness to make the second half of your life the best it can be.*

Turn on *Oprah* any day of the week and you can hear her or Gary Zukav or some Richard Gere–type celebrity telling you to let go of bitter baggage. *Baggage* is a common term in this new century. But how many of us really take the time or effort to create this vital turning point? Some of us wait until we get a fatal diagnosis or see someone close to us die clinging to old hatred before we change. Some of us are not sufficiently in touch with our own truth even to be aware of the hurt or bitterness we've carried into our everyday lives. The stories, exercises, and visualizations in this chapter are designed to help you get in touch with and release behaviors that no longer serve your well-being.

Hurt and Anger

We all have memories of loss, hurt, and regret. Most of those feelings present themselves outwardly as anger. Long-term anger becomes bitterness. You can't possibly be free to enjoy the second half of your life if you are nurturing resentful feelings. Now's the time to change it. Fulfilled women don't have fake smiles or pinched, angry faces.

~

Hollywood is full of offended people. There should be a special therapy group in Los Angeles entitled Canceled and Bitter. Marilyn tells of her brush with bitterness in that competitive world.

> When I was doing the NBC sitcom *The Mommies* in 1994, Drew Carey was also in a show on the same network. This was a year before his hit ABC sitcom. Every new season each network invites TV critics to Hollywood for a press conference in order to introduce their new series. When it was Drew's turn to promote *The Good Life*—a short-lived show starring John Caponera and Drew—he spent the better part of his time criticizing *The Mommies.* He said things like, "Wow . . . looks like NBC needs me—look what they put on . . . *The Mommies*. What? They couldn't find any real comedians? They had to go to the suburbs and get these two amateurs? They're a disgrace to women. What an embarrassment. I know hardworking, actually funny women who have paid their dues working the clubs for years who deserve a shot at a sitcom." He ranted on and on. And the worst thing was, everyone laughed with him. The whole room seemed to be in agreement that Caryl Kristensen

and I—The Mommies—accidentally and undeservedly got on national TV.

"Accidentally"—I agree. "Undeservedly"—that's harsh. I was embarrassed that Drew was making fun of us, and the humiliation was heightened because the critics and network executives were getting a big kick out of it.

The true feeling was hurt. The hurt quickly disguised itself as anger and indignation: Who is he to call us amateurs? What a pig! Then came the defenses: We paid our dues in other ways—motherhood ways!

Every time he was on television I urgently turned the channel. Our friends and family stood up for us to show their faithfulness. There was a little camp of suburban loyalists ready to pounce on Drew Carey if they ever saw him.

Time passed, and the angry feelings diminished. But the more success he saw, the more bitter I became. I never watched his show, and when others said it was their favorite, I cringed. I never saw him in person and didn't know what I would do if I did.

Then came the night of the big fight. The Tyson-McNeeley fight, that is. It was Tyson's first since his release from jail, and all the stars came to Las Vegas to watch the circus of events. Don't ask me what I was doing there. After the fight a lot of us went to this little restaurant to have a midnight dinner. Everyone was packed in so tightly we could hardly move. I was enjoying my appetizers when Caryl, who was sitting across from me, noticed that the back of Drew's chair was jammed up against the back of my chair. There had been so many people and activities, I didn't even know he was in Vegas. Caryl had a funny look on her face as she mouthed the words "Drew Carey" and pointed behind me. I was dense. I had no clue what she was trying to say. With more anxiety, she again mouthed and pointed. Perplexed, I slowly turned around just as he was turning toward me. Inches from his big face and with no time to think, I gave a little shocked gasp! And then blurted, "Why did you say those horrible things about us?" He hemmed and hawed for a moment and then said, "I was just a bitter, bitter man!" You see, he had been resentful because at that time our show had gotten picked up for a full season and his was only a midseason replacement. He said he didn't really mean it and suggested that we should have a barbecue together some time. Caryl was floored.

My hurt feelings have left, though I still let him humiliate me—in a new way. Every time I'm asked to do a commercial or participate in an event, I wonder if it's something Drew Carey will make fun of. I don't let those concerns be the deciding factor, but still, for half a second I do think about it. And sometimes I feel a little ashamed about my failures in Hollywood, compared to his successes. I'm sure in reality he couldn't care less, but the thought still pops in my head. Why I give him so much power, I don't know. But it's time I let it go, don't you think?

Like me, you may be righteous in your hurt and anger. My story is "hurt lite" compared to the real stuff life throws us. Emotions such as hurt and anger are part of the natural cycle of living. Anger is just a feeling. It's not wrong or bad to experience it. In fact, it's normal and healthy. Expressing your anger in an adult manner as it happens will keep you from exploding and will add to the sense of balance and well-being you want to experience. However, hanging on to angry feelings for months, even years will be destructive to you. At some point you might either blow your top at the wrong person, get physically ill, or implode. And, as in my case, old anger might transform into feelings of bitterness as well as shame or embarrassment. Why hang on when now is such a good time to do a reassessment and let go?

QUESTION

Marilyn let the opinion of one person eat away at her self-esteem.

Is there anyone in your life who has had that same effect on you?

Hidden Anger

As children most of us were taught to hide our anger. If we showed it, we were sent to our rooms or punished in other ways. As adults we might still be operating under the mistaken notion that anger is a bad thing. That doesn't mean the anger doesn't exist; it means we might just be hiding it from the rest of the world.

Ask yourself if any of the following things ever happen: You are fine until something unrelated reminds you of a bad incident or an offensive person. Or maybe an angry feeling simply appears. It could be triggered by something as simple as a song or a certain look on someone's face. Then you feel a wave of adrenaline, a tightening in your throat; your heart beats a little faster or your mood shifts slightly. Maybe you are unaware of what the feeling is, but you know it's uncomfortable. Our bodies are good indicators that something is disturbing. If you never talk about the original incident and never deal with it, the suppressed feelings can become destructive.

Trying to Escape Feelings of Hurt

When we get emotionally hurt we begin a series of ego-protecting behaviors so that we'll never have to experience those feelings again. In doing this we also prevent ourselves from experiencing all that life has to offer. At this juncture in your life we invite you to choose to stop safeguarding your ego and start living.

In this next passage Katerina, forty-seven, writes about how trying to protect herself from being hurt could keep her from enjoying a potentially fulfilling relationship.

HOW LONG DO I STAY HURT?

"Never tell your man how many guys you've slept with." That was the gist of the *Cosmo* article I read while sitting in foils under the hair dryer. "Why the big lie?" I thought. Then I remembered a time, not too long ago, when you met a guy and if you both owned a leather jacket and a Beatles record, you ended up living together . . . in less time than it took you to unzip his fly. Ironically, for all their impetuousness, some of those relationships lasted for years and ended up being important and meaningful. We were young and idealistic and we actually believed that "inhaling" would expand our consciousness and our understanding of the world.

I never saw myself as the kind of woman who would be without a man. I was never without a boyfriend. I knew how the game was played. I'd been well schooled in gender politics by two brothers and a formidable, albeit perpetually unfaithful father. Men liked me, and I liked them. I had a knack for finding great apartments and terrific men in Manhattan, where, according to my girlfriends, there is a shortage of both. Then came the guy who broke my heart and ground his cigarette in it. He was smart and charming and weak. And I was going to fix him. Of course it was impossible. That was the turning point. That's when I opted out of the mating game altogether. It took a lot of getting used to, but I managed and, some would even argue, blossomed. I had a career and a house, and I chose to have a child on my own. But there were nights when I felt that I would never get accustomed to the aloneness. Somehow, with the help of friends, who became my family, I eventually stopped feeling the need to be coupled.

I missed the sex. The body-to-body contact, the gift from the goddesses, the lotus fruit that begets the sweetness of temporary amnesia. . . . I remember reading about some European study that indicated that during orgasm women temporarily stop thinking about their children. Sex is the singular, primal, animal act designed by nature to beget life that is powerful enough to interrupt the psychic bond between mother and child. Mother Nature has a vicious sense of humor! More than the sex, though, what I missed most was the companionship, that sense that there are two, together and in alignment, to help each other to weather the storms, to carry the freight.

I find that the older I am, the more difficult relationships have become. Unlike in my twenties, I now require a two-page résumé of accomplishments just to drop my pants . . . even one time.

In a complete turnaround, and in a moment of strength and hubris, I began an affair with my contractor, who rides a motorcycle and lives in the San Fernando Valley. He is beautiful, ten years younger than me, and at the time was in pain over his recent divorce. It was supposed to be a fling; it wasn't.

Initially the relationship doctored my wounds. But in time life got in the way. His ex, my daughter, his family, the daily grind of complicated, divergent lives—nothing major, just routine roadblocks. I realized that I had been alone for too long, that I had become a bit like a feral cat. Craving contact but terrified of being held for too long, of being possessed and domesticated. I had become so skillful at leading that I had forgotten how to dance with a partner. Suddenly, his every misstep and minor infraction burned like a betrayal. Maybe it was because we were products of a different time and upbringing. Maybe it was because I had forgotten how to negotiate a relationship. In spite of our good intentions, we kept missing; we couldn't empathize with each other. It was the Tower of Babel, complete with psychobabble. It seemed as if we spoke a different emotional language. He couldn't understand how someone who was so powerful and in control of her life could at times, in the words of Bob Dylan, "break just like a little girl."

I couldn't understand why my young lover couldn't understand me. I would become hurt and angry at him, but more so, I was angry at myself. I didn't want to need him. I didn't want to want love. I was good at being alone. Yet this time being alone didn't seem like an option. I think it had something to do with hope. More specifically, it stemmed from the reawakening of the dream that love is still possible, even at this stage of my life.

Like many women of my generation, I am a complicated mass of contradictions. By some standards I'm considered somewhat low maintenance. I don't fuss much, and I don't need a man's name, his child, or his money. I'm not threatened by a man's career; I don't care if his best friend is a woman or that he spends time with his buddies. On the other hand, I demand respect, complete loyalty, and a commitment to personal growth. In other words, I expect to be cherished, to have my ass kissed . . . emotionally, that is!

In the words of French actress Jeanne Moreau, "I've got some lines in my face and I've loved every man who put one there."

After some soul-searching, I came to the following realization: What had kept me from loving was the fear of being hurt again. Like Pavlov's dog, which was first given food and then a shock, I had conditioned myself to expect that love would always be followed by pain. That's why every argument wasn't only about the particular problem my lover and I faced in the moment; it was also about injuries sustained in our previous bad relationships. In essence, I had spent years erecting an altar, a shrine to my pain. The shrine was designed to keep all men out except for the one who had hurt me. This was the cause of the drama with my lover. And although conflict and drama make for exciting theater, they make for lousy relationships. When I made this connection, I realized this: It was time to demolish the shrine.

That was more than two years ago. We didn't survive as a couple; our relationship became a casualty of our pasts. But we're both still here, struggling to find meaning, trying to be in each other's lives in a way that's comfortable and meaningful. It's not easy, because we're difficult. But I have hope. I'm certain that I loved him. I'm certain that I want someone in my life again.

I've lived life without love, and I've concluded that exiling your heart and your mind and your body for fear of being hurt is akin to starving yourself to death to avoid bad-tasting food. And self-starvation is neither a noble nor a courageous way to die. On days when I'm feeling as if I want to give up on love, I look at a piece of yellowing paper taped to my computer monitor. It reads:

Work like you don't need the money, love like you've never been hurt, and dance like no one's watching.

QUESTION

Katerina found that trying to avoid being hurt kept her from experiencing some of life's surprises. Once she let her guard down, she had the chance to get close to someone.

In what ways do you protect yourself from being hurt?

ACTIVITY: How Would Your Life Be Different?

This activity is another one better done in pairs, but it's fine to just read and answer the questions by yourself. If you are paired with someone, there are two roles to play. One person is the "storyteller," and the other is the "listener." Begin by reading all the rules; then choose who will do which role first. After you've completed the exercise, take a break and then reverse roles.

Storyteller: Think of a time in your life when you felt especially hurt. Tell your partner the story.

Listener: Completely sympathize with the storyteller. At no time should either of you try to fix the problem or even suggest things she could do (or could have done) about it. Just listen and say things like "That's awful" or "That's so sad"—whatever is most comfortable and appropriate.

Storyteller: Give as many details as you need to paint the picture.

Listener:

1. When she's finished, give a very brief synopsis of what you think happened, based on what you just heard.
2. Next, ask the storyteller how this experience effects her today.
3. Then pose this question: If you could choose to behave differ-

ently from this moment on—and it really worked—how would your life be different?

Take a break to let the storyteller compose herself.

Now switch rolls.

AN IMPORTANT NOTE: This activity is designed to encourage you to get in touch with your feelings of hurt. By telling your story to a sympathetic, safe person you should begin to feel some relief. You will also be examining how the hurtful incident remains with you and controls some of your actions today. This awareness is a very powerful tool and can be the beginning of a change in your reactions. Thinking about how your life would be different if you chose to let this hurtful experience go invites you to begin to heal.

Reconciliation

It's not always right to reconcile with the person who has hurt you, but it can free you from carrying around a dark heart. The second half of your life has so much potential. Why drag it down with old, negative feelings? This is the perfect time to let it all go.

It's an open-minded woman who can recognize the destructive actions of her parents and consciously choose another path. Suzy, fifty-four, writes about how she learned how to let go of anger by observing two family members.

> My father had it in for my brother's mother-in-law, and vice versa. The why and wherefore is as trivial and as easily forgotten as a schoolyard spat. The product of that vain, stubborn display is a terrible thing. My father refused to go to my brother's home. Ever. Intractable and inflexible, the man simply couldn't be swayed once he had formed his opinion. Loyalty was a big one for him, and if you wavered in your support he would draw a line through your name.
>
> By not going to his son's home he missed being a grandfather

to my brother's children. And they missed any guidance he might have given. I can't understand it now any better than I could years ago, when it started. My mother tried to turn him around and so did I and others, but he felt that my brother's actions put him in the mother-in-law's camp. For Christ's sake, the man was married to her daughter.

My father died without reconciling with his son. I learned a lot from Dad: how to let things go at the moment of affront in order to keep what's important to me intact, how to make peace for the sake of the bigger picture. To me, reconciliation means not looking back. It means forging ahead despite the past and working like hell to make change occur. It's always going to be incremental. And disappointment is probable. It helps, as well, if you don't have too big an ego.

I don't feel that it is necessary to reconcile with people who you don't give a hoot about. I feel you need to respond to your own inner voice. Do you miss the alienated person in your life? What was the real reason for the estrangement? Does that reason seem unimportant now? Is your vanity still offended? Well, get over it. What are you waiting for? Take that first step. The results might surprise you.

ACTIVITY: Freeze and Toss

This exercise is an old tried-and-true one frequently used by therapists and friends alike.

Make a list of any people you are still harboring any anger, resentment, or jealousy toward. On separate, individual pieces of paper write a sentence for each person, expressing the feeling you have for them. Example: "I resent my mother-in-law, Grace, because she is always meddling in my affairs." Now wrap each piece of paper in aluminum foil and fold it into a neat square. Place all your squares in a Baggie, then put them in your freezer. Visualize this: As the "Papers of Resentment" begin to freeze, their hold on you diminishes. Close your eyes and repeat the following: "With this symbolic gesture I let go of any resentment, anger, and jealousy, and therefore regain my power."

Three months from now, pull the packets from the freezer. Make up your own little ritual as you discard them. Say good-bye to those old negative feelings. Observe how those feelings faded as the pages froze; now that you've thrown them away, a refreshing new attitude will take hold and revitalize your life.

Payback

One way we keep ourselves in an angry place is to tell the offending story over and over, in hope that each listener will dislike the offender, too. Make no mistake here: It's a good thing to talk about it. In fact, when the episode first occurs it's very helpful and powerful to tell your side of the story. That way you gain some clarity as well as support regarding the hurtful incident. After a while, however, it's best to move on and let what happened in the past remain in the past. In other words, it's over. There are quite a lot of us who don't quite embrace that concept. We beat the story to a pulp. Have you ever found yourself getting energy behind telling your hurtful story even though it's been months, even years, since it happened? You begin to explain the story again, and once that door opens you get stimulated recounting all the wrongful doings the perpetrator has ever executed. Ask yourself this: Could it be that you're trying to *prove* that you were genuinely victimized and that the listener should feel sorry for you and choose to be on "your side"? Enough is enough. Yes, it's tempting to gather an even bigger list of people who agree with you. And anger, even old anger, does get your adrenaline going like a strong mocha latte. But is it supporting your goal of having a wonderful second half of your life? A good friend would say, "Well, I know that was very hard for you, and I agree that you were hurt, but it's time you put it to rest. Is there anything I can do to help you let it go?"

ACTIVITY: Smoking the Peace Pipe

Is there someone in your past with whom you have experienced a hurt or resentment and yet you kind of miss them? You miss their "good" side—the part of this individual that drew you to them in the first place. Would you like to reconnect with them but the old, hurtful incident is still looming in the way? Burying the hatchet can be a wonderful, freeing experience. If you'd like to give it a try, the following exercise will help.

First, complete the Freeze and Toss exercise (p. 78) with that particular person in mind. Then, calling upon your courage, make an effort to reconnect. Yes, write them a note, send them an e-mail, or even pick up the phone and give them a call. In essence, let them know that you have been thinking of them in a positive way and were wondering how they were doing. You don't necessarily have to bring up the altercation, but, knowing that it's the road to your personal growth, perhaps in time you will feel more comfortable doing so. Grab a good friend and tell her you want her support in doing this. Practice with her first. (Occasionally, our friends will try to "save our feelings" by talking us out of the reconciliation, but don't let them.)

You can also try this brave undertaking with someone whom you've had a misunderstanding or an altercation with but don't necessarily miss. Maybe you work with them or simply see them on a regular basis. If you bury the hatchet with this individual, you will enjoy the recovery just as much. Remember, it's for your own healing, *not theirs*. Nancy has tried this with a few people from her past and found that some interesting renewals of relationships have come out of it, leading to opportunities she'd never dreamed were possible.

Affirmation

From this day forward I have the power to change anything I want about myself.

Powerless

You have heard this next saying many times, but since this book is your wake-up call to take action, it's worth repeating: You give your power away to the very person who hurt you when you harbor deep emotions of pain and animosity. They *win* the game every time you put your life on hold, every time you overwhelm yourself with sadness, every time you feel sorry for yourself. These people are living rent-free in your mind. It's time to kick 'em out and take back your power. Make the future one where you, not your antagonist, are in control.

Creative Visualization: Take Back Your Power

(NUMBER THREE ON CD)

The following guided visualization has strong imagery to help release the part of you that wants to hold on to hurt and anger. It will prompt you to let it go, giving your conscious self the chance to reclaim your personal power. This visualization is designed to help the average woman let go of common anger and resentment; however, we are sensitive to any woman who has ever been a victim of incest, rape, or violence. Everyone heals in different ways and only when they're ready to face it. If you have ever had such a formidable experience, we recommend you seek counseling and talk to your therapist or minister about the notion of letting go.

Get into a comfortable position, either sitting in a chair, cross-legged on the floor, or lying down. Close your eyes. Begin to inhale through your nostrils and exhale through your mouth, gradually intensifying the deepness of your breath. With each inhalation, expand your stomach and chest, filling your lungs with air, and with each exhalation, empty your breath from your chest and stomach until they feel "collapsed." Do this very slowly. Breathe in through your nose to the count of four, hold your breath to the count of seven, then slowly exhale from your mouth to the count of eight. With each new breath imagine yourself pulling in positive energy and everything you need, and with each exhalation feel yourself letting go of negativity and everything you don't need in your life. Do this several times.

Picture yourself walking down a corridor. There are four doors along this hall. When you're ready, you will choose a door to open and you'll find a set of stairs. The stairs lead you down to a large basement. It's dimly lit, and you can see one person standing in the middle of the room. As you descend farther you see that it's a person from your past who has invoked in you feelings of jealousy, hurt, anger, or resentment. Picture him or her clearly. They are standing alone in the basement. This is your personal visualization, and you are perfectly safe. In fact, you can turn around and go back up those stairs at any time. Take a deep breath and muster up your fantastic courage. Do it again. Now picture this person wearing a red scarf around their neck. This red scarf is a symbol of their negative hold on you. Take another deep breath. In this story you are an adult and you have a lot of courage—you can call upon your courage anytime you want. Hold out your hand and tell the person they must give you the scarf. If they should happen to refuse at first, just keep your hand out and stare at them. Picture your perpetrator unwrapping the scarf and gently handing it to you. Take another deep breath. Say to them, "Thank you. As I take this symbol from you, I let go of any anger, hurt, or resentment I have toward you and therefore take back my power."

Now picture yourself building a fire in a small incinerator. It's a small, controlled fire—just large enough to burn a scarf, and the basement is very large. See yourself throwing the red scarf into the fire. See yourself saying, "As this scarf burns I am taking back my power." Feel it. The person from your past no longer has any hold on you. You and this individual are standing on either side of the incinerator, watching their old hold on you burn away to nothing. Turn to this person and look at them. Remind yourself that forgiveness is the key to your freedom. See yourself walking around the now dying fire in the incinerator, toward them. You are standing directly in front of them. If it seems right, embrace them. If not, that's okay, too. Repeat to them, "I choose to let go of any anger, hurt, or resentment I have toward you and therefore take back my power." Now picture yourself walking away from that individual. You're feeling serene, confident, and powerful, wearing a little smile on your face. Take a deep breath and repeat the following to yourself ten times: "I celebrate myself for the woman I am and I love the woman I am becoming."

In a moment you will come back to this reality feeling refreshed. Take three deep breaths. Notice the outside sounds. Breathing regularly, open you eyes.

Share

Whether you did this visualization alone or with your group, take the time to share your experience. Give as many details as possible. How do you feel now? Who was the person with the red scarf? Why that individual? How did their power manifest its hold on you?

If after you do this visualization or any other exercises in this workbook, you still feel uncomfortable, you might want to discuss your experience with a licensed therapist, a member of the clergy, or any other professional counselor.

Affirmation

I celebrate myself for the woman I am and
I love the woman I am becoming.

Another outstanding reason for letting go of bitterness is how it affects our health. When we carry hurt and resentment with us for many years our bodies absorb those emotions deep within. Sometimes they show up as chronic headaches or back pain. We clench our teeth throughout the night. We eat anything and everything to mask the pain. As we age, the future already threatens a natural decline in our health; wouldn't you rather enhance your well-being by letting go of the old inhibiting behaviors?

ACTIVITY: Peeling the Onion

Many times we'll think we're mad at someone for one specific reason, but in fact there will be much more information hidden beneath that anger. Once you can identify what the real cause is, you have the choice to be kind to yourself and understand your own feelings, and then work on the real issue.

According to Adlerian therapist Lynn Lott, MFCC, there are four common underlying issues. Read this activity through before trying it yourself and then see if you fall into any of the following four categories.

Justice: Deep down we think life should be fair. We carry a strong view of what is right and wrong (according to us). Some of the thoughts associated with the justice issues are "It's unfair," "Life is unfair," "It's not right to treat people that way," "People shouldn't treat people that way," and "I wouldn't do that."

Recognition: Sometimes we unknowingly carry a strong need for recognition. We feel inadequate if we're not properly appreciated. Some of the thoughts associated with recognition are "What did they think about me?" "No one noticed that I . . ." and "I deserve better treatment."

Power: Sometimes we want to control almost everything. We think our way is the best and only way. We want and need power in order to feel good. Some of the thoughts associated with power issues are "Nobody can do this to me," "I want it my way," "I feel powerless," and "I feel helpless."

Skill: Sometimes we think we are not capable of doing the task asked of us, whether it's making a difficult phone call or completing an assignment. We get angry because someone is pressuring us to follow through when what we really want to do is give up. Some of the thoughts associated with skills issues are "I can't do it," "It's not perfect," "It's never good enough," and "This is too hard."

After an argument ensues or angry feelings arise, try to "peel the onion" in order to uncover what's really behind the problem. Once you make that discovery you are invited to let go of the original dilemma and begin to work on the root of the problem.

When you do the following exercise you may be surprised at what truths have been quietly lying there. Do this exercise with a partner. Person 1 is the "worker"; Person 2 is the facilitator. Remember, answering "I don't know" is not allowed.*

Here's an example:

Person 1: I am angry at my friend because she quit seeing me for no reason. She's really weird. I didn't do anything. She just stopped calling.

Person 2: What about that makes you angry?

Person 1: Because she didn't make our friendship a priority.

Person 2: What about *that* makes you angry?

Person 1: Because friendship is precious to me and she just threw it away.

Person 2: What about *throwing a friendship away* makes you angry?

Person 1: Because I thought I was more important to her than I was.

Person 2: What about *that* makes you angry?

Person 1: Because I trusted her. I thought she liked me.

Person 2: What about *that* makes you angry?

Person 1: Because I feel abandoned and unloved by her.

Person 2: What about *feeling abandoned and unloved* makes you angry?

Person 1: Because I never do that. People shouldn't do that to each other; it's not right.

The answer "People shouldn't do that . . ." indicates that there might be an underlying concern with justice. Remember, this exercise is intended to determine what's beneath our hurt and anger; it's not designed to fix the problem. That comes later. For now, we're

*A note for Person 2 before you begin: Person 1 may become a little frustrated during the middle of the exercise. She may even bark at you, the mere facilitator. Don't let yourself get engaged. Have patience. It's not easy peeling an onion. Sometimes it makes you cry.

simply trying to discover what underlying issues might be at the heart of the feeling. What we might learn from Person 1 in the example is how important friendship is to her, how she lost trust in her friend and feels abandoned, and because she states that she "wouldn't do that," she may also be carrying a justice issue. If we were to ask her if a sense of unfairness has presented itself at other times, we would likely see a "theme" going on throughout her life. What may have started off as anger toward a friend for not calling can end up as an examination of something this person encounters fairly often.

Person 1: "I am angry at ________________________
because ____

Person 2: What about that makes you angry?
Person 1: Because ________________________________

Person 2: What about *that* makes you angry?

Person 1: Because ________________________________
Person 2: What about *that* makes you angry?

Person 1: Because ________________________________
Person 2: What about *that* makes you angry?

Person 1: Because ________________________________
Person 2: What about *that* makes you angry?

Person 1: Because ________________________________
Person 2: What about *that* makes you angry?

Person 1: Because ________________________________
Person 2: What about *that* makes you angry?

Person 1: Because ________________________________

You both will know when the exercise has run its course. Person 1 might get an "ah-ha" moment or simply run out of steam. Now patiently recap what you've learned about yourself.

If after you do this exercise, you find that you fit into one of the four categories, you can begin to break the pattern. It's only with awareness we can make the decision to change. You may also discover that the original "problem" you were so mad about has dissipated.

Cease the Need to Please

Most of our mothers were pleasing machines. They taught us well. One benefit of being a midlife woman in the twenty-first century is indulging in the knowledge that you can't please everyone anymore. Yes? Your experience has taught you this powerful axiom, and though it's been a hard one to learn, you've won the right to go about your business without fear of criticism. Right? If not . . . girl, it's time! Accepting that little piece of wisdom frees you up to experiment and discover a whole new world out there. A world you've been afraid to enter. A world of passion, creativity, and fun. A world that says, "It's not selfish to take care of yourself!" From now on, if you choose, you can experience the freedom that accompanies letting go.

Too often we try to please others because we're afraid of their criticism. It takes years to truly relinquish the need to please; but the first time, knowing that not everybody is going to like what you're about to do, you still go ahead and do it with confidence, you'll see that it's worth it.

~

When we try to please everyone in order to keep them from judging us, we spin impossible wheels. People will talk behind our backs no matter how angelic we are. It's their entertainment. It gives them the illusion that they are better than we are in this particular category. Let it go. JoAnne, fifty-one, writes about being so trapped in the "pleasing machine" that it got in the way of her family ties. Her poignant passage is included to help you stay on track when it comes to your priorities.

When I was in my late thirties I lived a contented life of making people happy. I made my kids happy. I made my parents happy. I made my neighbors happy . . . and my kids' teachers, the Little League coach, my hairdresser, the paperboy, and, once in a while, my husband. All I really wanted in return was for the aforementioned to like me—and for my husband to buy me a new dining room set. I had created a nice little world. Everything was status quo. Then something happened that changed my idyllic life forever.

There was one thing I hid from them. You see, my brother Marc was gay. Now, I considered myself to be quite an open and liberal person. I agreed with Phil Donahue about almost everything. I didn't have a prejudiced bone in my body. It's just that I wasn't completely sure everyone else felt the way I did, so why rock the boat?

My brother had always been on the feminine side. We had never discussed this; that way I could pretend it wasn't true. I prayed that no one else would notice. Heaven forbid that someone in my little world think of me as "the one with the gay brother." I figured (and here comes the quasi-liberal part) that what he did in his private time or where he chose to live was his own business. It was all fine as long as we never spoke about it. I found myself telling "gay" jokes around my brother, hoping to shame him into going straight. If that didn't work, at least I was giving him the message that I was not approachable on this topic.

Remember for a minute that I'm a "pleaser"; only in retrospect can I see that in order to please everyone else around me I had to "manipulate" the one nail that was sticking up from the board. I realize that what I was doing was wrong, and right now it's painful to be this honest. My brother was a very thoughtful and sensitive person. It kills me to think that I must have hurt him so much, but he never showed it.

Time passed, and I did a very small amount of "growing." Not a lot, just a little. Marc lived in New York and once, while he was visiting me, we finally discussed his lifestyle. I let him know that I loved him no matter what, but that "I wasn't ready to share this with my friends." (I said a *little* growing.) That special day we went for a walk, and we talked so much about the past and what he had come to accept and his fears. His biggest concern was that he did not want his nephews and nieces to think less of him because he was gay. I assured him that they loved their Uncle Marc and said that they didn't need to know right now, since they were too young to understand. When the time was right, they would be told, and they would still love him because he had developed such a wonderful relationship with them. This opened the door to my acceptance of my brother's life, but I still had the "screen door" latched. I wanted so much to be a better sister and rip that screen off. I just wasn't ready.

A short time after Marc went back to New York he called to tell me that he had met someone special and that he was moving to Paris. He also said that it would mean everything to him if I would accept his "new partner." I almost died when he asked me this; I immediately went back to "What will my friends think?" and closed the door again.

I could not even imagine my brother being in love with another man.

Things appeared to be going well for my brother. He was happy and studying architectural design. He always included Denis in his letters and phone calls, and I did not acknowledge that he was in a relationship with another man. I continued to live in my world and hoped he'd stay in his.

On November 11, 1992, at 7:04 A.M., my mother called me, sounding hysterical. "Marc is dead" were the words I could barely hear. She had just received a phone call saying that my brother had committed suicide. My mind went blank. I cried and then cried more. I prayed that I would wake up and this would not be going on. Unfortunately, I could not wish this pain away.

That evening I called my girlfriend Sandy to tell her. Then, to my horror, I felt a new shame come over me. I was embarrassed to say that Marc had committed suicide. I did not want her to think of him as weak. So I told her that he had died in a car accident. I can't believe I was still afraid of being judged at a time like this. She was consoling and supportive and said she would come right over. After I hung up I just sat there.

That's when it hit me. Here I was, grieving the loss of my dear brother, grieving what could have been—if only I had been open. Sorrow and regret were assaulting me, and yet I was letting my status with a good friend prevent me from being truly honest. There would be no step toward the healing process if I kept it all to myself. And for what? So I could look good? So that my good friend wouldn't know my brother was "weak"? I picked up the phone, took a deep breath, and called her back. I told her that Marc had committed suicide, praying that she would not judge him or me. I found her to be a loving and supportive friend, no matter what the circumstance.

The next few weeks were horrible, as we had to wait to have his body flown home. My entire family went to the airport together. That was the longest ride I have ever taken.

On December 4, 1992, the morning of my brother's memorial, I met Denis. I wasn't sure how to greet him. But the moment I looked into his eyes, I saw a mirror of my pain. I extended my arms and embraced him, not caring or thinking about other people's impressions. My brother's partner, whom I had not been willing to acknowledge before, was the one soul who would help give me strength through this difficult time. He was able to offer us much insight, peace, and understanding about Marc's final days. This gift I could never repay.

Denis stayed with us for a month following Marc's memorial and then had to return to Paris. None of us were willing to let him go. He gave us all a reason to wake up every morning. He had so much excitement to share. I discovered why my brother had fallen in love with him. I grieved for my brother hard. I gained some peace from hearing that he knew that I loved him, but at the same time I was full of regret that I had put limits on that love.

It has now been ten years since my brother's suicide. I still miss him, and I am thankful that I am not the same person I once was. This is the unique gift my brother has given me. Today I have the ability to be just JoAnne. And part of who I am is a woman who had a dear gay brother, and if there's anyone who's going to look down on me because of it, that's fine. It's their weakness, not mine or Marc's.

I wish I had been a better person while my brother was on this earth, but because of his love I am now able to love unconditionally; that is the gift I pass on to my children. And I have decided not to try to please every single person who comes my way.

QUESTIONS

JoAnne's compelling and honest story illustrates an extreme situation stemming from her need to be accepted by her friends and neighbors.

Is there anything you are keeping from people in order to prevent them from judging you?

If you had the courage to be real, what would you like others to know about you?

ACTIVITY: Say "So Long" to Servitude

As nurturing women, we often don't mind serving others. In fact, we quite like it. We're quick to meet the needs of our children, our mates, our parents, our friends, even our pets. When we give to others because we love them and want to show our love by taking care of them, it's a beautiful thing. When we find a kind of personal power behind doing things for others, that's okay, too. But when we do it out of habit, because it's expected, because we need people to like us, or because we're scared of receiving harsh consequences, it's an ugly thing. Having the courage to be real means looking at why you might be serving others and agreeing to do it only when you have pure intentions.

With a partner, list fifteen ways you currently serve others. List both the good ways and the bad ways. Have your partner coach you to really dig for the hidden ones. When you've gotten fifteen items, switch positions.

1. ______________________________
2. ______________________________
3. ______________________________
4. ______________________________
5. ______________________________
6. ______________________________
7. ______________________________
8. ______________________________
9. ______________________________
10. ______________________________
11. ______________________________
12. ______________________________
13. ______________________________
14. ______________________________
15. ______________________________

After you've both made your lists, go back over them and look for situations in which you gladly and willingly serve others. Put a "B.T.," for "beautiful thing," in front of those.

Next, put an "U.T.," for "ugly thing," next to the ones that make you feel resentful. There may also be some that are simply in the "neutral zone"; after those, put an "N.Z."

Obviously, B.T.s and N.Z.s are fine, but if you are overloaded with U.T.s, you've gotta change your ways, baby.

Add up your B.T.s and U.T.s. Figure out what percentage of the time you serve others with joy and how often you do your mandatory chores feeling unappreciated and resentful.

Now that the second half of your life is here, you can choose whether or not you want to continue this pattern. If you're ready to make a commitment to cease to please, read on.

With support from your partner, decide which obligatory actions you are willing to give up in order to become the real you. Circle the U.T.s. You don't have to give up all your ugly things at once, just start with one, then work your way through the list. Your family, your boss, your partner, your neighbors, and your dogs will all be okay if you are not their servant. Believe it or not, this is for the good of all concerned. There's nothing more frightening than a resentful woman doing you a "favor."

Enjoy your liberation from the "pleasing machine," for you have earned it.

~

When we get old enough or courageous enough—or sometimes both—we hit a defining moment in which we face the reality of a bad situation and finally say, "Enough is enough." As you read the following story, we encourage you to see if there's some sort of hurtful business going on in your life that you've been ignoring or maybe too afraid to really look at. We hope you can learn from forty-nine-year-old Charlotte and draw the line even sooner than she did.

ENOUGH IS ENOUGH

It was several days before Christmas when the Nordstrom's bill arrived. I routinely opened it, then noticed a charge that I had not made for an item purchased from the lingerie department.

My heart sank. He'd never bought me lingerie—at least not since the kids had arrived on the scene. I was sure my husband wasn't a cross-dresser; however, I had begun to notice subtle changes in him lately. He'd taken up running with a fervor I'd never seen before. He seemed distracted and easily agitated. He paid closer attention to his appearance, his clothing, and his haircuts. In addition, we hadn't had sex for two months. These were all the classic warning signs of a man having an affair, yet I remained cocooned in my own little world, not wanting to recognize them.

I pushed it out of my mind, sure that there was some kind of reasonable explanation—and on Christmas morning, I discovered just that! There, under the tree, was a big beautiful Nordstrom's box with a gift tag to me from Bill. There it was—the silk negligee that would have explain the charge.

As we gathered around the tree and it became my turn to open "the box," I realized how foolish I had been. How could this wonderful man betray his children and me? Surely he was simply on a "self-improvement" mission (which I could use as well), and I chided myself for doubting him. I removed the beautiful bow, raised the lid of the box, and pulled out the gift—a bright yellow rain slicker.

If I had gotten a rain slicker, then someone else was the recipient of the lingerie. And that became a turning point in our marriage.

Suffice it to say that the uncovering of the affair with Christine, his newest employee, was devastating.

I began therapy immediately. Thank God for Dr. Johanna. We also met as a couple every Saturday morning to try to determine if this marriage could be saved. Bill, faced with losing his family, readily participated. And so we tackled the task of rebuilding trust, confronting issues, and redefining the ways we treated each other.

I wasn't so sure this would work—after all, this was the second time in our ten-year marriage I had caught him in an affair. Therefore, the pressing question I had for Dr. Johanna was "When do you know when enough is enough?" What, I wondered, constitutes the breaking point in the marriage—one affair, two affairs, three affairs you're out? Her answer to my question was succinct yet simple. She said, "My dear, you'll know enough is enough when your integrity has been compromised."

How much would I be willing to take before I called it quits? At that point, the answer remained unknown for me .

Bill became completely committed to the restoration process of our marriage and swore off any further extramarital affairs. He became attentive, more loving, more fatherly to the children, and genuinely repentant for his sins. We worked together as a team to rebuild our lives and our family.

The commuting lifestyle didn't enhance the marriage, so we had decided that I would pack up the suburban house, move to Minneapolis with the kids, and we would all reunite in one place, under one roof, in the final act of solidarity. I got the kids enrolled in a new school, bought a terrific home on an appealing acre of property, and rented out our old home for the next two years to a lovely family from England. Over a period of two years, Dr. Johanna guided us to full and final reconciliation, and all was right with the world.

Until the phone rang late one night, waking me from a sound sleep. The clock said 11:45 P.M. The voice at the other end was unknown to me. A strange female—yet with a tinge of subliminal familiarity. She simply said, "This is Christine. Bill has been in a terrible accident and he's in intensive care. He's paralyzed from the neck down."

When I asked why she was the one calling me (after all, he'd sworn off her two years ago) she explained that she had been with him at the time of the accident. They were bicycle riding on the path on the lake when Bill's tire hit a patch of sand; he skidded and was catapulted over the handlebars. I fell silent.

That afternoon, after shopping for shoes for the children, Bill had explained that he had a big presentation due the following morning and had to return to the office to work. We had just had a glorious weekend, and my therapy had taught me to abandon the suspicious nature I might have assumed two years earlier. I'd kissed him good-bye and settled into an evening of making a back-to-school collage with the kids, showing how they had spent their summer vacation.

I sprang into Superwoman mode. I arranged for Bill to be transferred out of the substandard hospital where the paramedics had delivered him and into the best one in the city. I brought in a top team of neurologists, arranged for private nurses around the clock, and flew in his brother and sister-in-law for additional support.

Then Dr. Blinderman asked to see me privately. The news was devastating: Bill had suffered severe injury to the C-4 and C-5 vertebrae of the spinal cord. Until they operated, they would not know the exact severity of the injury, but the prognosis was not good. Time was of the essence, and they were preparing the operating room as we spoke. If the cord was not severed, they would need to get in there to release the compression on it immediately. It could make all the difference as to whether he would ever walk again. We agreed that together we would tell Bill what he was facing. As the doctor spoke, Bill's eyes filled with a combination of fear and tears. There was no turning back the clock. The moment of reckoning had arrived, metaphorically and realistically . . . for *both* of us.

As soon as the doctor left, Bill asked if Christine could join us in the room. I agreed to what could have been a dying man's last wish and called for her. She entered head down, never glancing at me, fearful of what our eyes might say to each other. She stood on the right side of Bill's bed. I took the left. Then, at the pinnacle moment of what could have been his last words, Bill proceeded to tell us how much he loved us both and to ask that the two of us not abandon him now.

The past two years flashed through my mind. Every ambiguity suddenly became crystal clear. I was married to a man who was so capable of living a guilt-free duplicitous life that on the possible brink of death, he had absolutely no contrition.

The time had come. I now knew the answer to that all-consuming question I had posed to Dr. Johanna: "When do you know enough is enough?" And, exactly as she had told me all those months ago, this was the moment *my* integrity had been compromised. It hit me between the eyes: If Bill couldn't find his way back to me in health, I knew he'd never find it in sickness.

I simply smiled, nodded, and touched his hand, brushing lightly over the absence of his wedding ring, then gently kissed his left cheek. It was time for surgery. They rolled him off to the operating room, leaving me standing directly opposite Christine—three feet of what used to be bed space between us—with a hole in my heart that felt at least that big.

Bill survived the surgery. The damage to his spinal cord was termed a "severe contusion"; the doctor reported that with any luck and lots of rehabilitation, he'd be walking in a few months. We were warned that it would be a long, slow process and that lots of family support would be needed. The last thing I wanted was to be held accountable for his not recovering—after all, he was the father of my two children, despite the anger and betrayal I felt because of him.

I knew what I had to do now, but doing it was another thing. I started with Christine. I invited her to join me for coffee in the hospital cafeteria, where I explained the plan: I would visit the hospital with the kids on Tuesdays, Thursdays, Saturdays, and Sundays. She could come on Mondays, Wednesdays, and Fridays. If anyone asked who she was, she was to reply "a close family friend." If I was to be locked into helping Bill get back on his feet (literally), I wasn't going to incur any further humiliation because of her presence. And that's how it went—for twelve long weeks. We each were there when he progressed from the bed to the wheelchair, albeit on different days. Then from the chair to the walker, the walker to crutches, crutches to a cane, and, finally, unassisted standing. The process of relearning to use your hands, your legs, and your bodily functions invites only those closest to you—and Christine and I were certainly that. Only at different times of the week.

Not once during those twelve weeks was there ever any discussion about the accident, about the infidelity, or about the duplicitous life he lived over the past two years. Yet to the hospital staff, to my children, and to Bill I was nothing but the dutiful wife supporting her husband's recovery process. Yet I knew what I had to do.

When the day of his release came, I did it. I picked him up at the hospital and drove him straight to the apartment I had rented for him, fully furnished with all his things. As I pulled up to the curb and invited him to get out of the car, he looked astonished. And I, knowing that enough was enough, finally felt free. Free of lies, free of pain, free of betrayal, and free of fear. I was ready to start the next chapter of my life completely free of guilt.

It's been ten years since the accident. During that time I was able to let go of any attachment I had to being "the victim." Sure, it took a lot of work, but it was well worth it. This chapter of my life has been the very best. I have been in a committed relationship for the past eight years with my life partner, Tony. He is my soul mate, my lover, my best friend, my business partner, and the love of my life. Over the past eight years he has helped me raise my two children and has shared with me the real meaning of a truly blessed, highly functional, monogamous relationship.

Bill and Christine married five years ago and have a new baby boy. I see them often and have actually become friends with Christine. I feel so happy and complete in my own new world that I simply don't harbor any bitterness. I must admit, though, that I do feel a little sorry for her. I keep wondering if she ever questions when he has to stay late at the office for big presentations the next day. Old habits are hard to break.

QUESTION

Charlotte is not alone in hoping for the best. Like any woman, she deserves to be in a relationship that boasts honesty, integrity, and kindness. This type of scenario can be translated to other unhealthy relationships—with friends, your coworkers, your teenage kids, your parents.

How much are you willing to take before calling it quits?

"Everyone's a Critic"

By now you've probably already lived through some of the worst criticism you'll ever have. It probably came from all directions—from your mother, your teachers, and your brothers and sisters when you were younger, and now you get it from your coworkers, your boss, and even your teenage children. Hey, if you've raised teenagers, you're ready for anything. We all know that a fifteen-year-old will condemn anything—from your choice of underwear to your personal style of breathing. Living with teenagers is like watching *Jeopardy!* every night . . . after a while you start thinking, "Maybe I *am* stupid." If you still have a budding teenager at home, here's a little tip from Marilyn: Go straight to the doctor and say, "One of us has to go on Prozac—you choose."

Living your life trying to avoid criticism is like trying to avoid the common cold—everyone is susceptible and there's no cure. Or as fifty-one-year-old Bev puts it:

> You'd think I would have gotten over agonizing about being criticized now that I've reached an older-but-wiser, tougher-skinned point in my life. However, it continues to be difficult for me to hear anything less than overwhelming praise for my accomplishments, be it over career, appearance, or character. Hell, I'm out on strike if someone doesn't think highly of my recent fabric choice for the kitchen curtains.

Remember the expression "Everyone's a critic?" The more crass claim, "Opinions are like assholes; everyone's got one." Avoiding criticism is futile, but when we're younger we really try to stay on that hamster wheel. Now that we're becoming goddesses, we can take it with a grain of salt.

Creative Visualization: Laughing in the Face of Criticism

(NUMBER FOUR ON CD)

If you haven't yet adopted this cavalier attitude, we're here to help. The following visualization is designed to give you some courage regarding criticism.

Get into a comfortable position, either sitting in a chair, cross-legged on the floor, or lying down. Close your eyes. Begin to inhale through your nostrils and exhale through your mouth, gradually intensifying the deepness of your breath. With each inhalation, expand your stomach and chest, filling your lungs with air, and with each exhalation, empty your breath from your chest and stomach until they feel "collapsed." Do this very slowly. Breathe in through your nose to the count of four, hold your breath to the count of seven, then slowly exhale from your mouth to the count of eight. With each new breath imagine yourself pulling in positive energy and everything you need, and with each exhalation feel yourself letting go of negativity and everything you don't need in your life. Do this several times.

Picture yourself in a familiar environment. Maybe you're at home, in your family room, your garage, or your studio—somewhere where you work on projects. Maybe you're working on something job related or you're cooking a gourmet meal or writing or getting ready to go out. You are simply going about your business when you realize there's a critical person standing behind you. They make a snippy little comment about you. What's your reaction? Whatever it was, that's fine.

Now let's create this scenario again. You're working on whatever project you were doing originally. You're content with what you're doing, enjoying the process. You realize that there's a critical person standing behind you. They make a criticism about how you're doing this task. This time you turn around slowly and smile. You say to yourself, "Oh, here comes that pesky critic again." The critic makes another biting statement. You continue to go about your business, thinking, "Man, this poor thing has *got* to get a life." Your critic is relentless. When you look at them you notice that they're slightly smaller than they were a minute ago. The negative remarks aimed at you begin to get a little more sharp, a little more personal. You watch the critic's face twist up as they spit out their comments. You smile again when you notice that the critic is simply shrinking. Now they're about the size of a toddler. Their voice becomes high-pitched as their size diminishes. This critical little person continues ripping on you and all that you stand for. The more they keep barking at you, the smaller they become, until they're about the size of a peanut. You bend over, pick them up, and put them in the palm of your left hand. This jerk's still going at it. You can barely hear them now. As they continue to point out all your weaknesses, you take your other hand and . . . flick them out the window.

At that moment you see a bird swoop down and pick up your little critic. The bird flies away and you go back to your project, humming a little tune. After a while you complete the project and repeat this affirmation to yourself: I am a clever, capable person and I don't care what anybody else thinks.

In a moment you will come back to this reality feeling refreshed. Now take three deep breaths. Notice the outside sounds. Breathing regularly, open your eyes.

Share

Whether you did this visualization alone or with your goddess group, take the time to share your experience. Give as many details as possible. How are you feeling now? Who was your critic? What was your first reaction when you saw them? How did you feel when they kept shrinking?

Again, if at any time you experienced uncomfortable anxiety, explore this experience further with a trusted therapist, member of the clergy, or any professional you trust.

We Are Our Own Worst Critics

Self-criticism is one of the most detrimental habits we can have. Now that you are in midlife, make a huge effort to stop this destructive behavior. Bev shares her turning point.

Criticism doesn't stop at what others think of us. When we who are chronically unsure of ourselves in the first place allow even a wee bit of criticism in, it opens the floodgates of our own low-self-esteem-tainted insecurities!

Haven't we all been successfully convinced by now that we are one-of-a-kind special in this world? When the dark clouds are allowed to sweep over our heads, this uniqueness can also be viewed as a lonely, barefoot stumble down life's often rocky road. We know our strengths, but at the same time, who else but yours truly knows the bottomless depths of our weaknesses?

Self-criticism has got to be self-flagellation at its most painful. That inner voice we hear can cripple us emotionally far worse than anyone's opinion. It can expose our fears and vulnerability like nothing else and no one else can. So how can we turn this negative act of exposure into a positive move toward growth? I began tossing around this question: What if I chose to accept and nurture that vulnerability rather than trying to sweep it back under the proverbial rug? Dealing myself a gentler hand is a kindness long overdue!

This enlightenment is a present I've recently given myself. The "high" is longer lasting than buying a new pair of shoes or another appliance for the house. It enables me to "lose the 'tude"—and work without being critiqued, one baby step at a time. I can give myself a break and at the same time learn tolerance for others' shortcomings.

With each new day, I can now look forward to more of these liberating steps that contribute to the greater ideal of self-love. I'm learning to accept my imperfections and accept me for the delightful creature that I truly am—endearing flaws and all. Armed with the knowledge that there is always room for improvement, I can appreciate my strengths and do some creative work on my weaknesses, allowing myself to move on with living something of this precious, exciting, and oh-so-imperfect life.

QUESTION

What about yourself do you find the easiest to criticize?

ACTIVITY: Talk to the Kid

Bev's epiphany is significant; that critical inner voice can be damaging. That's where using the technique of self-talk is powerful. One way to get in touch with the part that's reminding you of your shortcomings is to imagine that it's the child in you who's doing all the clamoring. Visit that ten-year-old you and tell her that she's just scared about something. Comfort her the same way you might your own children. Tell her not to be so damn hard on herself. Use some of your grown-up wisdom to make her feel better.

You can do this spontaneously or meditate on it. Either way, it will work. Sometimes we need to be reminded to feel compassion for our own child within.

Affirmation

I am a clever, capable person, and I don't care what anybody else thinks.

Letting go of old behaviors that are not providing you with a sense of calm freedom or a feeling of excitement and appreciation for life is the best thing you can do for yourself at this turning point. When we consciously or unconsciously move about our daily lives carrying hurt feelings and bitterness, when we fear others' opinions and serve with resentment we sabotage our chances for true happiness. Each of these destructive behaviors are hard to root out and it may take our lifetime to do it, but not trying or ignoring them will keep us frightened and unfulfilled. Take inventory now and use this new awareness to make the second half of your life the best it can be. The more often you revisit this chapter, the more you will get out of it.

Chapter Four

Turning Point No. 4: Shore Up Spiritually

YOUR MOTHER'S MIDLIFE: *For a woman of our mothers' generation, "spirituality" was synonymous with organized religion. She probably continued to practice the religion her parents brought her up with, went to services each week, and put money in the offering plate. Most likely, the God she worshiped was thought of as an all-powerful male deity who punished us for our sins. Prayer may have helped her through a souring marriage, the loss of her parents, and the loneliness of the empty nest.*

YOUR MIDLIFE: *In our midlife, spirituality has its place as well. A personal definition of a positive and nurturing God replaces the idea of a God who was to be feared as well as worshiped. And we discover that our mothers may have been onto something when they realized that faith heals.*

As we are pressed to face the highs and lows of the second half of life, one sustaining force that can give us comfort and courage is our spirituality. Having none can cause the uneasy sense of free-falling. To shore up spiritually means to put in place that belief system, that ritual, that philosophy which speaks to your soul. It's our individual attempt to give and receive comfort, to make sense of what life has given us, and to aid in the effort to make the world a better place.

Getting in touch with your spirituality doesn't necessarily require going to a place of worship every week, although it may involve that for some. Here's where it's different for others of us: There seems to be a new outlook regarding religion these days—and there's a concomitant sort of spiritual tolerance women of our generation have for one another. Sure, there will always be fundamentalists and zealots, but the general atmosphere in more hearts says that a person can be spiritual in whatever form they wish to. It's as individual as hairdos.

A woman's spiritual journey may not involve organized religion at all. What seems to be the common thread for most women who consider themselves spiritual is finding a "practice," or combination of practices, that can soothe them in times of turmoil and help them on their road to self-acceptance in a world that seems to offer less and less enjoyment in the physical realm. For others, a traditional approach is comforting. The familiarity of fellow worshipers meeting each week to reinforce a strong belief in God and helping one another through hard times is exactly what a lot of women still need. Both ways bring you down the same path—trust in and comfort from knowing that there's something bigger than all of us. And that there's some divine order to the universe.

Let's face it: The times when you can cheer yourself up by going out and buying that trendy little outfit or eating a big wedge of chocolate cake are becoming scarce. As the years go by, the things that used to seem so crucial to your well-being, like looking good and making a lot of money, become less important. Life events become symbols of our own waning mortality. That "forever" marriage ends, your best friend becomes ill, your child is using drugs—all these events signal a time for your own life review. How can you get back to the peace of mind you had as a trusting child? Revisit your spirituality.

Finding Your Own Path

Nourishing your spirit might involve communion with others, found in the camaraderie of a church or a synagogue. Or you might walk a solo path, your pew a log in a cathedral of redwoods, the sounds of the birds your only choir. As is so often the case, many midlife women find their spiritual path when they admit that they are powerless over their lives. Suddenly, when they are feeling burnt out, tired, sick, and without hope, it comes to them—like a light in the darkness. Nancy's midlife crisis renewed her desire to find some spiritual meaning in her life.

MY OWN BACKYARD

This wasn't the first time I'd gone searching. Only now that I was in my forties and faced with unbearable hardships, I suddenly felt desperate to know that there was something good and true in this existence that can sustain us against all odds. Something that connects us to one another as human beings, and to a life force that is greater than all of us. I wanted to know that I could grow and become enriched by life's challenges. I needed a spiritual answer to the question "Why is this happening?" As a new string of hardships surfaced in my life, I realized I needed "shoring up" on the spiritual level.

I began by revisiting many of the same pursuits that had given me comfort before. Only this time I found what I was looking for in my own backyard, as clichéd as that may sound.

For me, that comfort comes from a place that I have known since early childhood, and it's my personal source of magic. Horses were my passion for as long as I can remember. From the moment I laid eyes on those beautiful creatures, I was awestruck. I realize this doesn't sound like anything one might associate with spirituality, but for me it is just that. In the softness of their big brown eyes, the curve of their cheeks, the flare of their nostrils, I see the magnificence of creation. I can finally relax. When I watch them move, I am moved. The intertwined smells of saddle-soaped leather and hay, the sight of sunlight hitting the beams of the barn, and the touch of a muzzle are incredibly comforting to me. Out on the trail I take gratitude and prayer as seriously as a Baptist minister. A family of red-tailed hawks circle in the thermal winds and call to one another and I am reminded of miracles. In the presence of horses, I am a humble, reverent human being. I say a prayer for them each day, and express my gratitude to my creator for putting them in my world.

QUESTION

What or who brings you comfort in times of trouble?

ACTIVITY: Finding Comfort

By taking a look back and reflecting on that which has comforted us before, we can often unlock the key to the positive things that will guide us in midlife. Find a quiet time to sit and meditate on the people, activities, and traditions in your life that may nurture and renew your spirit today. Have a group discussion or do some journal writing regarding this; then answer the following question:

Is there a way to incorporate them into your life now?

~

Comfort and spirituality come in many forms. This chapter is designed to help you see that there are a number of ways you can get back to being a spiritual being. When we open up to all the possibilities, we open ourselves up to new ways of receiving comfort. Like Nancy, in her search for help and enlightenment Sherry discovered that the worst of times brought about the best of changes.

ZEN AND THE ART OF FLY-FISHING

By my late forties I'd run out of energy, ideas, and, eventually, hope. My mother had suffered a stroke, I'd been in a serious car accident, and my creative arts school had been hit by a tornado. Soon after I'd resettled and restocked the school, the landlord more than doubled the rent. For the first time, I considered walking away from a business I'd worked fifteen years to create. I left my office, turning the decision over to a higher force. The next morning, from out of nowhere I got an offer for the kind of space I'd always wanted and the chance to design it myself. With our busiest season approaching, the timing was critical. Every day before work I brought doughnuts to the crew, trying desperately to keep things on track.

The building was finished on time, but I was burning out. I was supporting family members, employees, friends, and students. But while I kept everyone else happy, I was sinking into depression. My blood pressure shot up, I had to go on medication, and my doctor announced I'd have to make changes or I would die.

I didn't know who I was anymore. In trying to be what others wanted of me, I'd lost my soul, my spirit, and my love of life. I sought help from a therapist and stunned my staff by leaving to spend five weeks in a cabin in the Colorado mountains. I was going to fly-fish and find my soul. I packed books by Thomas Moore, Joan Borysenko, and Caroline Myss, Tao books, relaxation books and tapes, writings by the great mystics, and some good music. The spiritual quest was on.

Being outside, immersed in the elements, had always been important to me. Before fly-fishing, gardening had connected me with nature. Digging in the dirt or standing in a stream makes me feel whole. It's like being held and comforted by something vital to my life, and it gives me a true sense of belonging.

I returned from my trip transformed. I knew my relationships would have to change or I could be in crisis again. It was a hard transition, both on me and on everyone who had relied on the "old me." Being "the boss" in a business and in a family takes its toll. It's like working without a net. I used to feel that no one could catch me if I fell. In truth, when I allowed the fall, I was caught and gently placed on the ground. Now when I feel there is too much to shoulder I hear a voice saying, "Boo, go fly-fishing," which translates to "It's time to say no." So much of life boils down to *trust*. When I get out of the way . . . the way is there.

Your God, Your Way

God is an intimidating word. Like *spirituality* and *religion,* it has a personal significance for each of us. Because of a strict religious upbringing, some of us grew up with a definition of God that doesn't ring true when we reach adulthood. In most cases, the God of our childhood was an all-powerful male deity who was judgmental and vengeful. While the words of a favorite good-night prayer may have comforted many children, other kids were filled with terror by such lines as "Now I lay me down to sleep; I pray the Lord my soul to keep. If I should die before I wake, I pray the Lord my soul to take." And then there's the football player who thanks God for the win—as if He has the time and power to give or take away the game.

Some of us who want "God" in our lives know it's the best way we can pass on love, but we need to go on a search for a definition that feels right for us. Occasionally we don't find that until we enter midlife.

Barbara, fifty, shares her experience of finding God.

"WITH GOD ANYTHING IS POSSIBLE"

I am a baptized Catholic. I graduated from parochial grammar school and attended catechism classes during my high school years and for many years following. God was religion, and religion was ritual with a list of dos and don'ts. As a young adult, I became disillusioned when I found hypocrisy in the church members, and I left to do my own thing.

Let's face it: We all have difficult times. By the time I hit middle age I really wanted something spiritual I could resonate with. I certainly needed something outside of myself to hold on to while struggling with the work of relationships or parenting concerns. And when doctors didn't have the answers I wanted to hear, I had to look elsewhere for solace while loved ones fought with their health problems. As a self-employed business owner, I was often faced with many business confrontations and related financial woes. What made all of these struggles even more difficult is that fact that I am a perfectionist. I'm even proud of it—I consider it quality control. I am full of the highest of expectations for myself and those around me. However, this only added to my stress and caused me to be unhappy and unsatisfied.

Then I discovered Cursillo, an ecumenical four-day retreat weekend that is held in a cloistered environment where it is safe to share fears, expectations, and difficulties about all of the above. It's a weekend full of music, prayer, stories, and community support, and it ends on a very high note with everyone chanting, "With God anything is possible."

I found people there who have survived their own worst fears. They taught me that God is "love" and is available to us right where we are at this present moment. My teachers are not experts, only people who have the courage to look beyond themselves for a power greater than they are. I could hear God in their words and see Him in their actions. I began to learn more about this power that is greater than I am by listening and watching those fulfilled people. I knew in my heart that this religion was right for me.

The best part about the whole movement is that we can take a piece of it home to our everyday lives, reach out to those around us who are hurting, and pass it on as needed. There is no specific ritual that I must adhere to—only a strong belief that this power of love is available.

I have since studied the Bible and different types of prayer, which further adds to my description of the God who is ever present and soothing to me in my every need. I am certainly much happier knowing that there is a positive choice I can make, rather than reaching for my seat on the pity pot.

Then there is forty-one-year-old Therese, who finds that the old traditional meaning of God and the church values she was raised with resonate more clearly than ever with her today. She recalls when REM's popular song "Losing My Religion" seemed to be becoming an anthem for a generation of soul searchers—with the exception of herself.

NOT LOSING MY RELIGION

It seemed that everyone around me was searching for answers, mostly women in my age group (somewhere between the baby boomers and Generation X). They tried everything, and formal religion took a backseat or was wholly discarded. Was this the backlash of catechism and years of religious dogma or just part of the wanderlust of the 1970s and big money of the 1980s? By the time the '90s hit, we were all exhausted by the search, and most of us had given up. REM struck a chord in '91 with their hit "Losing My Religion," and it was no longer fashionable to be a card-carrying Catholic, let alone one who still attended mass regularly (and not out of guilt but—gasp—desire).

I do not spend my life thinking that all good deeds in life lead to a heavenly reward; nor do I believe that all negative actions are a one-way ticket to hell. I can only tell you that I find comfort, solace, a sense of community, and continuity in a crazy world through my religion. And it is my religion. This is not my parents' religion, nor is it the strict doctrine of fifteen years of Catholic education. I've taken what works for me and personalized it.

As I find myself at a crossroads (you know the standard one: personal fulfillment versus professional success), I'm even more reliant on my faith to help me make the right decisions for my life. Believing in my faith helps me believe in myself, that I can achieve my dreams and goals. A good friend recently described me as "fearless," and I attribute that trait to my faith, to that constant compass that guides me.

ACTIVITY: What Does Your God Look Like?

This exercise is designed to help you see the many individual forms "God" can take. It helps if you have someone be the designated reader of this activity.

Get into a comfortable position, either sitting in a chair, cross-legged on the floor, or lying down. Close your eyes. Begin to inhale through your nostrils and exhale through your mouth, gradually intensifying the deepness of your breath. With each inhalation, expand your stomach and chest, filling your lungs with air, and with each exhalation, empty your breath from your chest and stomach until they feel "collapsed." Do this very slowly. Breathe in through your nose to the count of four, hold your breath to the count of seven, then slowly exhale from your mouth to the count of eight. With each new breath imagine yourself pulling in positive energy and everything you need, and with each exhalation feel yourself letting go of negativity and everything you don't need in your life. Do this several times.

Go back to a time in your childhood and picture yourself at Sunday school, temple, church, or wherever you first recall learning about God. Try to recall some of your first impressions of the word *God*. Did you first hear the name in the words of a sermon or a prayer? Did your mother or father, or maybe your grandmother, describe God to you? Did you see pictures in a book or painting? What image does this conjure up for you? Get a good picture in your mind of what you thought the image of God was. Does this image still hold up for you today?

Now, just for a minute, we're going to expand our vision from the first impression to something else. Think of this God as a force of nature. For you, would it be sunshine? Wind? Earth? Perhaps your interpretation of God is in the roar of the ocean or the quiet calmness of a forest. It could be more than one phenomenon. Take a minute and choose the force of nature that best fits your feelings about God. (If someone is reading aloud, she should pause here for a while.)

Think of this same God as a feeling. What name would you give this feeling? Love? Strength? Comfort? Joy? Perhaps you associate some other, different, personal feeling with the word *God*.

Now envision yourself at your happiest, during one of the peak experiences in your life. Perhaps this is a tender moment with a loved one. You have never felt so happy—so at one with the world. Now picture that God is with you during this experience. Imagine God as a force of nature, then as a feeling, and then as a person.

In a moment you will come back to this reality feeling refreshed. Take three deep breaths. Notice the outside sounds. Breathing regularly, open your eyes.

Share

Write about what you have just experienced. What did your God look like as a force of nature? As a feeling? As a person? Compare your images with those of your group. How are they different?

~

A difficult challenge can be a path to a new spiritual view of your world. Nancy's battle to have a child gave her a new perspective on trusting her "higher power."

LEARNING TO TRUST

In the beginning of my effort to have a child I would often ask myself, "Why is this happening, God?" But I was afraid to ask God the question because—God forbid—He might say, "Ha! I'll show you!" First came the diagnosis of my husband's prostate cancer and, with it, the realization that I could only conceive a child biologically with him through in vitro fertilization. (For those of you who don't know, the removal of the prostate means a man is shooting blanks.) This was followed by a visit to the fertility doctor and the discovery of a cyst on my ovaries and severe endometriosis—the so-called career woman's disease. My first in vitro attempt followed, and of course it failed, because my stress-wracked body refused to get pregnant.

We turned to adoption early and were thrilled to be selected right away. I took the fact that I got the call from our adoption attorney on my birthday as a spiritual sign. We brought the young couple out from the Midwest, ready for the delivery of our baby in just a few weeks. But this situation brought frustration once again. It wasn't a match—the drugs, abuse, and insanity in their backgrounds scared the hell out of us!

I begin to doubt that I could keep my intention alive in the face of such failure. My husband, understandingly disappointed each time, covered his frustration with questions of doubt about our becoming parents.

We hit upon a new solution: Find younger eggs to implant in me from a younger woman. Once again, I attacked this plan with my customary drive and gusto. I was in my element, producing again, certain of a successful outcome. I found a deep spiritual connection with the young woman I selected as my egg donor, as well as with her family, and I saw this as yet another sign that this time my mission was on the right track. My friends performed fertility rituals around me before, during, and after the procedure. Marilyn even made a special necklace by hand for me, with a Madonna to wear around my neck, and lit fertility candles in my room during my forced twenty-four hours of bed rest. Staying in bed an extra day for insurance, I prayed and visualized positive thoughts about my soon-to-be-born baby. I felt so pregnant, I was sure it was twins, and I even picked out names for them, girl and boy.

The week of waiting before the pregnancy test was sheer torture. Now I felt it was only a question of whether there was not just one but two babies inside of me. I called the doctor at the appointed hour. The results were negative.

My friends went with me to Mexico to visit orphanages, where I was sure I would find an unwanted baby to adopt. But the process was far more difficult than I'd imagined, and friends and officials alike warned me to abandon the idea. So we decided to go back to domestic adoption, and within weeks we got a call from the adoption attorney wanting to know if we would take a Mexican baby—a young birth mother had called and wanted to give up her soon-to-be-born daughter.

I flew to Phoenix to meet "Jennifer." She held my hand as she looked into my eyes, tears streaming down her face, and told me how much it meant to her to know that a couple like us could give this baby the life she couldn't.

But there was no baby girl. "Jennifer" turned out to be a scam artist who wasn't even pregnant. She conned us out of thousands of dollars, stole our rental car, and shattered our faith.

How do you get that faith back?

I don't really have the answer to that. All I can say is that when the moment comes, you know that your higher power was looking after you all along.

On September 11, as I was watching the World Trade Center collapse, the phone rang. That was the day I found out about the young birth mother who was to bring our baby into the world. That was the day I learned never to give up on my faith.

Spirituality and Tragedy

A spiritual foundation can give you a way to cope with the inevitable tragedies that come our way in this lifetime. For some, the level of tragedy is incomprehensible. It raises the question "How could there be a God if something this horrible can happen to someone so good?" But from just such situations arise many of the world's greatest achievements and personal missions, as well as a renewed sense of purpose in life.

Scott and Catherine are close friends of Marilyn's who experienced a great tragedy—the loss of a baby. But with their dedication to their church and their personal spirituality, they turned it around in the most extraordinary way. As you read their story as seen from Marilyn's perspective, think of what a lonely journey this could have been without the comfort of prayer.

SHANE'S INSPIRATION

They had been the golden couple, with a long-lasting, strong relationship, an exquisite wedding, and a planned pregnancy conceived while honeymooning in Italy.

I think I enjoyed their pregnancy almost as much as they did. My grown children are slow on the draw when it comes to producing babies, and I had been craving a little one in my life so badly that I'd started treating my Chihuahuas like they were newborns. After a healthy nine months, both our houses were vibrating with love for and anticipation of their newborn baby boy.

One evening I got the call from a mutual friend, Laura. "Catherine had the baby," she said.

I shrieked, "Oh my God! When? How is she? How's Scott? How's the baby?" To my horror she answered in a somber voice: "Not good." I held my breath. Through her tears, Laura explained that the baby couldn't breathe on his own and that he was paralyzed from his little nose down. My family noticed that I was crying and gave me the "What's wrong?" signal. Not ready to say it, I ignored them and continued to listen to Laura describe the perfect birth and then the moment of shock.

Laura and I tried to think of ways we could help Catherine and Scott, but we were totally powerless. We both were hanging on to the hope that there'd be some expert right there at Cedars-Sinai who'd know just what to do.

That's all you can do at first, you know. Just rely on the hope that there's someone out there who can fix it. In the beginning, you are not capable of thinking about the alternative. You shut that thought out as fast as it comes in. Then you pray.

Each time I got a call from Laura, the news was worse: "Shane has a rare genetic disease that's not curable."

"The baby can't live on his own."

"They have to take him off life support, but Scott and Catherine can't decide on which day to do it."

My heart broke with each call.

My thoughts and prayers were with Scott and Catherine. For me, part of the praying process is to ask for help with acceptance of those things that I cannot change, and to find the strength to stay in the present in order to be there for someone else. Please understand that I was losing a baby, too. And that though my loss was nothing compared to the loss Scott and Catherine were facing, I needed to honor it nonetheless. I was already in love with Shane and all that a newborn promises. I had been waiting for my turn to baby-sit, to hold him and smell the babiness in his neck, to spoil him with the latest stuff, to giggle at his made-up words, to smile at his description of his first-grade teacher. I'd thought I could get my "baby fix" with Shane.

Almost two weeks after the birth, Scott called to invite my husband and me to see Shane before his death. I felt extremely honored and a little nervous. The pain of losing a beloved child is one of the hardest things to see registered on a friend's face. I'm sorry to say I've seen it twice before. Again I prayed for strength.

It was a quiet ride over the hill to the hospital. Richard and I walked pensively down the corridors toward their room. I saw Catherine first and flew to her, while Richard did the same with Scott. I wanted so badly to console her, and all I could do was cry with her. Big, bellowing sobs. We stood there hugging for a long, tender time. I could feel the warm protrusion of her belly where Shane had been protected all those months. Her breasts were full of milk. The pump next to her bed screamed the word *emptiness*. I noticed that the frame of her body seemed even smaller than I had remembered.

I don't think I had ever heard a man cry the tormented way Scott was. I wiped his tears with my hand, but there was so much more.

That brief time right there in that hospital room was one of the most intimate occasions of my life. It's easy to be a friend when it's all about parties and vacations and even long, revealing talks. The other side of true friendship comes with once-in-a-lifetime moments, like those we shared that sad day. I didn't think it could be possible, but my love for both of them multiplied.

We followed them to the intensive care unit, where little Shane lay breathing with the help of his machine. This is where I saw an amazing change come over both Scott and Catherine. Their melancholy expressions disappeared once they entered the room. During their short time with their precious newborn, they were very proud parents. They were joyful and delighted. The nurse helped Catherine hold him in a rocking chair with a portable breathing apparatus. She cooed and sang and told him how much she loved him. Scott took pictures and pointed out all the ways Shane resembled his mom and dad. Shane looked beautiful in Catherine's arms, and she looked beautiful holding him.

The next time I saw them was at the funeral. The same people I had seen at their wedding not even a year before were now gathered for another reason. This ceremony was as elegant and beautiful as the one before. Shane had been cherished and honored.

At the grave site I stood next to my husband, and my ten-year-old daughter, Marcy, stood in front of me, engulfed in my protective arms. The look of anguish on Scott's and Catherine's faces was so compelling, I whispered in my daughter's ear, "See their look? See the pain on their faces? I'm sorry, honey, but we all have to experience it at some point in our lives. There's no getting out of it. It's the natural way of things."

That's the harsh truth of it. Death is part of the life cycle, and I wanted my daughter to know about it because I think somehow it's easier if we know beforehand that it's the way things naturally are.

Then I said to her, "Look around and see all the friends they have. That's the best you can ask for in times like these."

So that's the sweet truth of it. The healing we receive from friendship is also an integral part of nature's cycle. Supported by their friends and family, Scott and Catherine clung to their belief that God had a mission for Shane.

A couple of years later, Scott and Catherine were blessed with a baby girl. They're smitten with her. She's the perfect combo of her mom and dad. Meanwhile, Scott and Catherine have turned their grief over the loss of baby Shane into a wonderful charity in his name. Through their tenacity, a lot of fund-raising, and hard work, they created what is called a "boundless playground," where handicapped children can play alongside other children. If Shane had lived, he would have been restricted to a wheelchair, and their compassion for children who need special help goes way beyond their grief. It took them four years to complete Shane's Inspiration, as the playground is called, and they're currently working on a third playground. They've been honored by the city council and the mayor of Los Angeles several times.

The Strength of the Spirit

Anna, forty-nine, has always believed that life has sent her plenty of blessings and that her spirituality has helped her deal with the tough times. She really relied on those values twelve years ago, when her spirituality came into play during an extraordinary circumstance.

Except for some morning sickness, Anna's second pregnancy was pretty smooth. She already had a five-year-old son, she was in good health, and her doctor didn't anticipate any problems. Yet when their little girl was born, she and her husband were hit with horrendous news. In the womb, a cancerous tumor called a neuroblastoma had attached itself to the baby's liver. Mom and baby Kate were rushed to Children's Medical Center, where they put Kate in the neonatal intensive care unit.

This was the beginning of a nightmare that would last almost two years. The doctors recommended chemotherapy as the best treatment, but because Kate was an infant, they could only guess at the amounts she should get. Kate was in and out of the hospital as her health alternately improved and weakened. One afternoon, Anna and Kate were at the hospital for an appointment when Kate suddenly stopped breathing and turned blue. Doctors rushed to revive her, then cut way back on her chemotherapy dosage. If they hadn't been in the hospital at the time, Kate might not be around today. Thankfully, the chemo was successful, and around her second birthday Kate was declared cured. Today she is a gorgeous, happy ten-year-old.

The time she spent with pastoral counselors at the hospital, together with the death of her mom a few years later, crystallized something for Anna. Raised a Catholic, she had a strong spiritual belief system and a desire to help others. But since the Catholic faith has not taken the leap to allow women in the priesthood, Anna had to make some important decisions. After talking everything over with her family, Anna enrolled—at age forty-one—in the Perkins School of Theology at Southern Methodist University.

She graduated first in her class and received a rarely given award as a future female church leader.

Today she's an ordained Methodist minister, although she's holding off on leading a church of her own until her son graduates from high school. Next year she plans to go back to school to earn her doctorate in pastoral counseling. As she moves into midlife she wants to share with her community the strength and peace that spirituality can bring.

How is it possible to come through such traumatic experiences as Catherine's and Anna's with a renewed sense of faith? A belief in the immortality of the human spirit can comfort us. Psychologist Darlene M. Graeser, Ph.D., conducted a study of terminally ill AIDS patients and concluded that spirituality helped them cope with their anxiety about death. She suggests that these patients, having learned that they were terminally ill, turned inward to seek meaning in what was inevitably a deeply disturbing experience. This parallels the research of Viktor Frankl, whose beliefs about man and life originated from his own experiences in Nazi concentration camps. He argued that people can find meaning in even the most painful suffering, and that life becomes meaningful only through what we take from it, what we give to it, and the stand we take toward a fate we simply cannot change.

Practical Spirituality

A spiritual belief system can help midlife women cope not only with the extraordinary challenges presented by tragedy but with the challenges of everyday existence as well. The juggling of motherhood and career has been endlessly documented, and it is of no surprise to most women that they are under far greater stress than their partners in managing both work and family. Putting her spirituality into practice is one way Nadine, forty-five, balances her life. Her positive outlook is not what you would expect to find in the cutthroat world of Hollywood. But that's exactly where she was introduced to the form of Jewish mysticism known as the Kabbalah, at a group gathering in a friend's home.

LIVING THE KABBALAH

My study of the Kabbalah has taken me on a journey and given me a new way of seeing things. I now know that if I have absolute certainty in my life, I will find the strength I need. I am on a path. Instead of being the effect, I can be the cause. I can be active instead of reactive, and I can be the light instead of the darkness. And in place of chaos, I can substitute simplicity. We are all here for a reason, we are all vessels, and how we fill that vessel is up to us. They say the Kabbalah isn't the light at the end of the tunnel; it is the light that burns away the tunnel itself.

Creative Visualization: Walking Your Own Path

(NUMBER FIVE ON CD)

The following visualization is designed to give you confidence in choosing which road you need to take to make your unique brand of spirituality right for you.

Get into a comfortable position, either sitting in a chair, cross-legged on the floor, or lying down. Close your eyes. Begin to inhale through your nostrils and exhale through your mouth, gradually intensifying the deepness of your breath. With each inhalation, expand your stomach and chest, filling your lungs with air, and with each exhalation, empty your breath from your chest and stomach until they feel "collapsed." Do this very slowly. Breathe in through your nose to the count of four, hold your breath to the count of seven, then slowly exhale from your mouth to the count of eight. With each new breath imagine yourself pulling in positive energy and everything you need, and with each exhalation feel yourself letting go of negativity and everything you don't need in your life. Do this several times.

Picture yourself riding on a bus. It's comfortable and warm, with big pillows and blankets. The sound of the motor helps keep you in a sleepy, relaxed state of mind. There are only three other people on the bus with you, but from your vantage point you can't see who they are—and yet it feels comforting to have them there. Everything feels calm and serene.

A soothing voice comes on the loudspeaker, telling you that the bus will be stopping at different locations in the most beautiful part of the desert. The voice says that you will instinctively know which stop is yours. The others have already gone on their journey. It's your turn now.

The next stop is the most stunning, and when the doors open you feel a warm and comfortable breeze gently blow your hair. As you step off the bus you see three paths, each leading in a different direction. One is made of soft, flowing grass; another is of smooth, colorful stones throughout a warm little stream of water, and the third is a tree-lined dirt road. Choose a path and begin to follow it.

Your path eventually leads you to a large, smooth rock on a bluff overlooking a magnificent canyon. The sky is giving you several shades of blue, pink, and orange. It's warm, lovely, and comfortable on this lookout. Sit on your rock and take a deep breath. Soak in all the abundant colors, the warm breeze, the smells and sounds. Feel the gratitude of being alive in this wondrous world. Now say a prayer. It can be a prayer of thanks, a request, a wish, or a prayer for someone else. Whatever prayer you say will be the perfect one.

When you are ready, return to your path. On your way back to the bus you see the other people who have chosen the other paths, and everyone seems serene and satisfied. You all meet at the bus and climb back on. As the bus leaves this beautiful place, you know you can go back as often as you wish.

In a moment you will come back to this reality feeling refreshed. Now take three deep breaths. Notice the outside sounds. Breathing regularly, open your eyes.

Share

Whether you performed this visualization alone or with your group, take the time to share your experience. Give as many details as possible. Which path did you take? Why? Did you recognize any of the other people? What was your prayer?

If for any reason after you do this or any other exercise in this workbook you still feel uncomfortable, you might want to discuss your experience with a licensed counselor or clergyman.

~

Finding a personal definition of a spititual leader can be as significant for our spiritual development as finding a personal definition of God. Nancy talks about her favorite guru.

> When I think of the greatest guru of all for me, and I emphasize *for me,* I realize it isn't some maharishi or mystic but my wonderful grandmother Diddy. After her death, we found her well-worn Bible, with this verse taped inside the front cover:
>
> *I looked for my God, I could not find him.*
> *I searched for my soul and it eluded me.*
> *I reached for my sister and I found all three.*
>
> That verse explains my life's true calling. When I feel I have lost my way, reading those three simple lines gets me back on track.

Midlife is a time for courage. Many difficult passages will be coming our way, and if we strengthen ourselves spiritually, we can take it. Today is the perfect time to get in touch with or get back to the spiritual voice that calls you. You may have to redefine what you were taught as a young girl, embrace it even more than before, or discover a new way to look for enlightenment and find comfort. Whichever sits right with you is good. Shoring yourself up spiritually readies you for the bumpy road ahead. It's an important turning point that will guide you through the darkest moments and touch your mundane daily existence with the spark of the divine.

Chapter Five

Turning Point No. 5: Get a New Perspective

YOUR MOTHER'S MIDLIFE: *Our mothers' generation believed in the homogeneous way. From prom queen to Donna Reed, it was all about fitting in! Differences were scorned, not celebrated. If she was brave enough to do it her way, she paid a high price.*

YOUR MIDLIFE: *Vive la différence! Today's woman is a mix of different cultures and backgrounds. We know that being unique is a blessing—no one has our individual look, style, or attitude—and we like it that way!*

Which of the following statements fits you best?

I've led quite a boring life compared to my friends'.
I'm saddened by all the tragedies that have come my way.
My life has been great and it's only getting better.
I've experienced so many disappointments in my life.
I've had some ups and some downs, but nothing spectacular.
The highlight of my life was when I was in college—nothing compares to it.
It's not about my happiness—it's about my children's happiness.
My career has sustained me through all the bullshit.
My life would be complete if I had a mate/child/divorce/boob job.
In my heyday I was on top of the world.
If only ______________ (fill in the blank), then I would be happy.

Did you notice that there's a pattern to these statements? Each comment falls into one of two categories: good or bad. At this turning point we invite you to rethink how you view the events that have formed your life so far.

Start by envisioning your life as a tapestry woven with colorful memories. We said *colorful*—not just pleasant. Colorful is what makes you the unique woman you are today; pleasant makes you boring. Nobody else has the background, the smile lines, the education, the hurtful memories, the joyous moments you do, and every little variation is what makes you unique. If your goal in life has been always to be happy, you've probably been unhappy much of the time. Be conscious of the fact that it's not only the positive experiences that shape us into the sage we are to become; it's the "full Monty." If you shift your perspective, holding off judgment regarding the "good things" verses the "bad things" that have happened to you, and accept that they are all part of the uniqueness you've derived over the years, it will help you achieve a strong sense of freedom.

You can get this new perspective on the events of your life by passing them through the "unique" filter instead of the "bad" filter. If you switch off the negative attitude, your experience will be peaceful and fulfilling. But, you ask, how can I change the way I think? It takes some work, but it can certainly be done. We recommend that you shift your perspective by practicing some of the exercises in this chapter.

Nancy was lucky enough to receive this gift, which she shares with us:

DIDDY'S FILTER

Growing up with a younger brother with Down's syndrome was not easy. Usually when I tell people about it they express sympathy. When I was younger, kids would tease me for having a brother who was a "retard." Back then I'd get so upset; I couldn't understand why they would be mean to such a wonderful soul. My grandmother Diddy—my guru, my muse—told me that those kids were simply too ignorant to understand the way life really was. In her soft, southern accent she explained that my brother David was a "love child put on this earth for the soul purpose of giving and receiving love, and only special families had the privilege of experiencing this."

I'm so grateful for having such a sagacious grandmother, with her unique way of seeing things. Now, in midlife, without trying to be somebody's Pollyanna, I try to interpret the experiences of my past through a sort of "Diddy filter." In almost every circumstance I can see how that experience—what many people would perceive to be negative—has in fact made me stronger and wiser. Most importantly, these experiences have made me uniquely me and have shaped a part of my personality that is compassionate and tolerant, and for that I am thankful.

ACTIVITY: The Diddy Filter

Write down five life-altering experiences—or turning points—you have had, both good and bad. Try not to judge them. Just write down what comes to your mind first.

1. ____

____

2. ____

____

3. ____

____

4. ____

____

5. ____

____

Now go back over your list using the "Diddy filter." Think in terms of how your experiences have made you stronger, kinder, braver, wiser, or more aware of others. Ask yourself how these experiences helped to create a completely unique you.

A Brief Overview

Sometimes encapsulating what we brought into each decade helps us remember what makes us different. If we break our lives down into ten-year segments, we can get a quick perspective on some of the situations within an era that made us who we are today. Leaving out judgments as to whether one decade was better than another and slightly generalizing the "theme" of each decade will help you form a new opinion of who you are now. Here's an example of this technique using Marilyn's life. You can see that these summaries don't necessarily depict her life as good or bad—they're just her particular take on those decades.

MY TWENTIES

When I was twenty I was a tree-hugging, pot-smoking hippie chick. I was not a true free spirit, though—you know, like those girls who danced at every chance possible, picked flowers and stuck them in policemen's hats, let their body hair go its own way, and had babies underwater. Not me, I had to shave my underarms, and though I did let the hair on my legs grow, I bleached it. You might say that in my twenties I was a shallow hippie chick.

MY THIRTIES

I can remember being thirty and realizing that I had pretty much turned into . . . I can't say it. You see, one hot evening I was sitting out on my front porch in my Kmart lawn chair beside a couple of friendly neighbors, each of us holding a martini in one hand. My minivan was parked in my freshly cleansed driveway, while my kids jetted past me on their Big Wheels. We were eating bean dip I'd made from this new recipe out of my Tupperware bowl—with tortilla chips in its "Modular Mate"—and I believe I was complaining about taxes when I stopped midsentence. Oh my God. I had to ask myself, "What's next? An RV?" Beads of sweat started forming on my forehead. I could hear a voice in the distance chanting "You . . . are . . . exactly like . . . your . . . mother." As if in slow motion, I ran into the house, lit some incense, and meditated for about twenty minutes. There's no place like ommmmmmm. Then I ordered something from my Lillian Vernon catalog, permed my hair, and continued my suburban way through the eighties.

MY FORTIES

At forty I was an assertive role model for those who wanted to learn how to snap at someone. I'm not exactly sure how I got there, but the pendulum had swung far away from the people-pleaser me. Passiveness gave way to assertiveness, which eventually gave way to aggressiveness. Add a couple of mouthy teenagers, a midlife crisis, PMS, and hemorrhoids to the mix and you've got dy-no-mite. My family could clearly see I needed a little guidance. I began therapy, revisited all my New Age techniques, got a good handle on my priorities, gained a little perspective, and near the end of my forties I found my favorite new drug—Prozac. Some people began to say I was wise; others said I was crazy. I took both as a compliment.

MY FIFTIES

I'm halfway through fifty now, and I feel a freedom like never before. I couldn't give a damn if a person wants to judge me. Have at me, I say. Criticism doesn't have the old hold on me it used to. I've gotten over my aggressive stage—one might even say I've "mellowed out." Another thing: I've been looking at RVs lately. I still love a good tree, though I'm no longer compelled to hug one. I'm dropping antacids instead of acid. I'm a little more jaded and a little less idealistic. I still laugh at everything. I don't take all my clothes off in public anymore. That would be so wrong. At my age, you don't want to be wagging naked body parts at people. See why some people say I'm wise?

ACTIVITY: Ten Years at a Time

Following Marilyn's model, write a short descriptive paragraph for each decade of your life, beginning with your twenties. It doesn't have to be earth-shattering—just a few lines about who you've been and what phases you've gone through.

When I was in my twenties I______________________________

____

____

When I was in my thirties I______________________________

____

____

When I was in my forties I______________________________

____

____

When I was in my fifties I______________________________

____

____

When I was in my sixties I______________________________

____

____

When I was in my seventies I____________________________

____

____

Playtime Activity

Have a "Girls' Night Out," where you and a few fun friends meet at a bar, restaurant, old haunt, or someone's house and do a night on the town—each dressed as you were in your favorite decade. You can surprise one another with your choices, or you can all decide on one wild decade (like the sixties or the eighties), or you can each represent a different decade. Make it even more fun by giving each person the assignment to come up with a "surprise." This can be an old boyfriend popping in, an unexpected visit from an out-of-town girlfriend, getting hold of an obscure song, or any fun thing you can think up.

Are Your Hardships Something to Be Proud Of?

Kurt Hahn, a philosopher and the founder of Outward Bound, helped many people find a new perspective by teaching that "your disability is your opportunity." We believe that this is an important point for any woman in midlife to embrace. No one illustrates it better than Oprah Winfrey, who revolutionized the television industry by fearlessly forging ahead in her mission to enlighten and entertain women during the daytime. After early career struggles, she was eventually championed by an executive named Dennis Swanson, who believed in her because of her distinctiveness. He realized that millions of women would indeed relate to Oprah because they saw themselves reflected in her image. We embrace her because of her warmth and her humanity, not someone's narrow-minded idea of what a talk-show host should look like. Oprah is a true rebel. She takes those negative experiences and uses them to help heal others. When she told her stories of having been sexually abused as a child, she made many women feel that they weren't alone. When she shares her weaknesses and insecurities, she makes it acceptable for all of us to reveal the details of a shameful past, which in turn propels the healing process. What brought Oprah to this point of compassion and what makes her unique are the various experiences life handed her and the decisions she made along the way.

We all have that same opportunity.

ACTIVITY: Let the Hard Times Work for You

This activity is a difficult one because we're going to ask you to look back to a part of your life that brought you pain. Take a minute and think about one of the worst things that has happened in your life. Just one will do. If you have the courage, share this information, with as many details as you can summon up, with a person you trust. Do this exercise even if you've talked about your event many times before. When you've completed that part of the instruction, have your partner help you uncover some of the things you have gained from this experience. It might take you a while, or a few rounds of practice, to come up with something positive from this painful incident that has helped you to become the kind of person you are today. Then answer these four questions: Concerning this ordeal, what about yourself can you feel proud of? Have you been able to help others who share your type of experience? Do you want to begin helping now? How would you begin?

Rearranging Your Negatives

This doesn't happen all that often, but every now and again a bitter, judgmental person will make a biting, negative remark about your passion, your talent, your looks, or your parenting skills. Occasionally we'll take such insults to heart and begin to criticize ourselves. At this turning point, we'd like you to look at some of those remarks that might have been thrown at you and find a way to turn around these adverse judgments and get them working in your favor. Here's an example from thirty-six-year-old Joelene.

MAKING WARM AND FRIENDLY LEMONADE

I had been doing voiceover commercials for radio for the past four years. Not an easy accomplishment, considering that sometimes it takes many years just to get an agent to represent you, let alone landing the work itself. Lately it had been a struggle.

About six months ago my agent dropped me because he said my voice was "too warm, soothing, and pleasing." At first I thought he was somehow praising me. After all, those were the same comments I'd received for the past fifteen years on the complimentary side of the ledger. But the sneer on his face as he spat out the words indicated that he no longer thought my warm voice was good or marketable. Needless to say, I was devastated! I was depressed. I was disheartened.

I shared my disappointment with a group of friends, who immediately jumped on my bandwagon. After cursing my "stupid" agent, they suggested that I consider looking at this as a positive, creative business idea rather than a confirmation of a dead-end career. We brainstormed through dinner and came up with a product idea that combines the positive aspects of my voice with my entrepreneurial and selling skills and my desire to help people. This group of inspirational women helped me get the confidence and trust to continue and persevere, despite setbacks.

I've known for many years that I wanted to give my voice as a gift to people—thus my baby, Voice Magique, was born. Through research and feedback I've created personalized, warm and soothing audiotapes that specialize in comforting babies, helping children and teens cope with problems, and supporting and nurturing women. Some tape topics include: building self-confidence, socialization, achieving your dreams and goals, feeling safe and loved, and the first day of school. They're all done with (and I quote my ex-agent here) a "warm, soothing, and pleasing" voice!

The business has become extremely successful, and I'm grateful to have the opportunity to help people, using the talent that God gave me; to experience turning something negative into a positive; and to pursue my dream! I'd like to thank my former agent, my many supportive and wonderful friends, and my clients, who listen to me.

In Search of Your True Self

Through the years we have added to and changed our personalities to fit the needs of each situation. It's part of our survival instincts. Within all those built-up layers of the "tough you," the "victim you," the "independent you," and the "pleasing you," there may be a few personality traits that you resonate with more strongly, now that you have lived a little longer and have become a little wiser. Chances are, those hidden—or some not-so-hidden—aspects are part of the "true you." Perhaps you are someone who receives personal comfort when you nurture things like your garden, animals, or friends. Maybe there's a highly competitive side of you that comes out at company picnics, in the car, or at the cookie bake-off. Maybe you are a poet. Maybe you see art in the most simple things. The authentic you is something you came into this world with—it's an affinity for certain things or lifestyle behaviors. It's never only one thing, but a variety of characteristics that make you feel "right" and "at home." When we get in touch with our authentic self, we nurture something unique about ourselves—something to be honored.

Nancy discovered something about her past she wants to incorporate now. She's using her new perspective to embrace something that she enjoyed about herself in the past.

REBEL ROOTS

Sometimes I look back at my career years and see a woman who wore power suits and high heels and became a vice president in a male-dominated company that made both nuclear reactors and television shows. She was hungry for approval, power, and status. Today I ask myself, "Who the hell was that woman?"

Before those years I was a rebel—from the time I was a toddler. It's funny how I lost that wild child for a couple of decades, but I guess it had to do with the need to please and win acceptance. Yet I love the rebel in me—the girl who got kicked out of school for smoking outside by the flagpole and then tried calling the ACLU on the grounds that it was wrong because school hadn't started yet. The girl who on Flag Day got in trouble again—this time because, protesting the use of the school's Confederate flag and calling it a display of racism, I brought in a homemade red one with a sickle and hammer on it.

I was the kind of girl who knew every word to every Doors, Stones, and Zeppelin song, who thought Abbie Hoffman, Gandhi, and Martin Luther King were cool. Who, surrounded by a pink-and-green sea of prepsters in khakis and topsiders, sported studded jeans and platform shoes.

So now in midlife, I have a new appreciation for that rebel child. And as I mature I am returning to those roots. I am much more likely to don a fringed suede jacket and jeans than a power suit, my ideas are still left of center, and I still think Gandhi is the coolest. I am done with waking up with a cup of strong coffee, my mind churning about the competitive hours ahead of me. Instead I breathe in some fresh morning air, take a long ride on my horse, and kick ass when I see a Confederate flag.

I hope I always feel a bit like an outlaw because it's who I am.

ACTIVITY: Who Are You?

Describe yourself as though you were receiving an introduction before giving your famous speech entitled "Appreciation of One's Personal Uniqueness Can Be Liberating."

Ladies and Gentlemen,

About to enter this stage is a woman who ________________

____

____

____

____

____

____

Physical Uniqueness: Getting a Perspective?

Trying to look positively at the changes to our bodies and skin now that we're at the midpoint is a challenging task. Battling time can be strenuous. At what point do we accept the natural ripening process, look at our double chin as "unique," and show off our sagging knees? Some women remain the plastic surgeon's friend a little too long; others are eager to show off their laugh lines. One's response to aging is as individual as it gets. Sure, it's easy to say, "Applaud your physical uniqueness—look at those enlarging jowls with a new perspective!" It's another thing to actually do it.

Madison Avenue advertising agencies are in the business of enticing the populace to their product by using the most common denominator: sex. They present us with what is supposed to be the most desirable look a woman can achieve—young and sexually ripe, with pulsating ova. And what do we do? We buy it. We buy it all—

the product, the look, the status, everything. Forget that this excellence is not attainable for most of the population at any age, leaving us real people with a feeling of being doomed with thin hair, thick ankles, crooked teeth, straight eyelashes, crow's-feet, pigeon toes, and only one or two good eggs left.

The Madison Avenue look is imagined. Nothing about it is real.

Looking and feeling authentic is such a great feeling. When we embrace our uniqueness, we give ourselves the freedom to be loved for who we are.

Even if some of us have managed to evolve spiritually, we can still slip easily into that shallow area regarding how we look. All too often we forget the joyfulness and pride awaiting us when we view ourselves as being "one of a kind." Marilyn talks about trying to get a grip regarding her physical image now that it's been on the earth for more than fifty years.

MARILYN ON GETTING A GRIP ON MY IMAGE

Sometimes when I get out of the shower I accidentally look at myself in the mirror. I don't see my body, or even my mother's body, I see my roly-poly, pasta-lovin' Italian grandmother's body. It's hard to appreciate your figure at any age—nobody ever does—but now that I resemble Noni, it's really a challenge. I look back at pictures of myself from just five years ago and ask, What was I complaining about? And it's only going to get worse. By worse I guess I mean deformed . . . or reformed.

And then there's my face. If my eyes weren't so bad, I would happily avoid the dreaded magnifying mirror. Gasping, I quickly moisturize—especially my neck. If I forget to grease that thing up, it looks as though I already have a scarf on. I have noted on several occasions that I have the same neck skin as my Chihuahua.

After a nice tweeze of the big black hair coming out of my mole (I love that—it's like fishing), I still succumb to trying to look younger by wearing blush. Blush? At my age I make others blush. The uncontrollable gas alone is enough to embarrass even the dog . . . you know, the one with a neck like mine.

Luckily, lately I've been able to change my perspective a little. I'm getting a better grip on what's realistic for a woman in her fifties. Sperm-friendly? Come on. First of all, I'm not about to make any more babies. So I figure nature is just doing its job by making the one who can no longer procreate a little less glowing, while my offspring have become the ripe, throbbing ones. Their sperm and ova need no synthetic boosters or yam cream.

I'm still married to a very dear husband, whose elbows give away his age, too. I ask myself, "Why would I want to try to allure someone else? So I can remind myself I'm still sexy? And that would help my life in what way?" For an old married woman like me, trying to win a new male's approval by dressing like a tart and displaying seductive behavior to soothe some fragile, aging ego (mine) would not make me more lovable. In fact, it would set me aside, make others uncomfortable, and keep me in the groveling position. It's just television and magazines that make me think I'm not good enough unless I can tempt a penis.

When I contemplate the image I truly want to portray, it's not a thirty-something vixen but a fun, "together," artistic individual who enjoys who she is.

Don't get me wrong—I don't mean that middle-aged women have to be asexual. Playful flirting at any age is a good thing—that is, when it comes from a centered, confident place—and whether you are married or single. It's when you turn yourself into something you're not that it goes south. A single woman in her fifties who exudes warmth, intelligence, and humor is the most alluring thing around, no matter how much weight she's carrying or where her breasts hit her.

QUESTION

What message do you think you give out with your image?

What image would you like to have?

At what point do we just let it go, let it "all hang out"? Acceptance is one thing; giving up is another whole ball of wax (the kind of wax you can heat up and line your upper lip with, and thus prevent your lipstick from seeping).

Jan is a fifty-two-year-old single woman. She lives with her big white dog and is a happy human being. She's also torn.

THE HELL WITH IT

Part of me wants to maintain my place in the world of the young and sexually active. I want to flirt. I want to wear pretty clothes and fuss about my hair. I want more of those long, slow first kisses.

Another part says, The hell with it—I've had enough. I don't want to starve myself every day to stay thin. I don't want to build my day around my exercise schedule. I don't want to jam my feet into high heels. I don't want to wear tight clothes that force me to stand up straight and suck in my stomach. In other words, I don't want to fight it anymore.

The problem is, society says we're supposed to fight. Otherwise, we're giving up—letting ourselves go. It's barely permissible to *get* old; looking old is certainly not allowed. When we say that an older woman looks "fabulous," we mean that she looks young.

Worrying about how we look shouldn't take up so much of our "I'm Not Good Enough" time. What makes us unique has to do with so much more than the house that holds the soul.

~

Some of us are reminded of what we used to have, and now lack, by a young daughter with nice taut skin who sashays around our kitchen while we eat what she left on her plate. If you don't happen to have one of those sweet, young, thin things at your fingertips, you still won't get relief, because chances are that you have a television. Getting a new perspective also means getting honest with yourself. Forty-seven-year-old JoAnne came to grips with herself one day at the mall.

DON'T COMPARE

I guess the most difficult thing for me to accept was that I've aged enough not to get those second looks. I love hearing people tell me that I look so young for my age. I figure either my friends are sucking up to me or the vitamin C cream I learned about on *Oprah* is working.

The other day my sixteen-year-old daughter and I went shopping. I had spent some time, as I always do, dressing nicely, taking pride in my makeup and hair—and of course I used my "Oprah cream."

As the two of us were walking through the mall, three good-looking teenage boys strolled by, looking my daughter up and down. As a mother I wanted to grab them by the balls and demand, "What are you looking at, Squirt?" Instead, I just smiled at that thought and kept walking.

That evening I mentioned this story to a male friend. I was explaining how I wasn't thrilled that she is at this age when he interrupted with "Are you sure they were checking out Jamie?" For just a brief moment I paused, thinking, "Could it have been me?" Then he started chuckling. That little deflated balloon went whirling through the air, disappearing as quickly as my waistline had. At that moment I had to accept how foolish I was to even consider that these young boys would look at me twice. As I blushed I thought, "My God, JoAnne, get a grip and grow up!" Then he said, "I'd take a woman with your sense of humor and a clever mind like yours over a sixteen-year-old's figure any day." Ah, a new perspective! I thought, "My God, JoAnne, it's good to be grown-up."

Native Americans say there are four stages of life, like the four seasons and four directions. Being a child, a young adult, a middle-aged adult, and an elder each brings a teaching, and each is equally important. Youth is for learning, and aging brings wisdom. Native American women have a different perspective about aging because it is not thought of as a problem, but is natural and respected. Fifty-five-year-old Carlton has adopted the Native American teachings and brings her perspective to our book.

FOUR SEASONS

I was raised in mainstream American society, but I have renounced the mind-set that most Americans have about aging. I prefer to think like Native Americans, to give respect to all parts of my life. Life is about putting energy into things no matter how young or old we are. I realize more and more that it is what we believe in and where we put our hearts that gives us strength at any age.

In my forties I became involved with the Lakota tradition and their ceremonies. I started doing sweat lodge ceremonies and helping with vision quests. I also started learning the Lakota ceremonial songs. In my fifties I was invited to a Sun Dance that was being held here in Arizona on the Navajo reservation. I started by supporting the dancers for several years, and eventually I was asked to participate in the dance as a cedar woman. Cedar is a purification element that all the dancers are smudged with during the dance. The dance is held only once a year, but there are also four pipe ceremonies, held in each of the four seasons. The dancers and helpers come together to smoke the pipe and pray for the earth and for the people. Even though it is a five-hour drive for me and even farther for some of the other dancers, we come to these pipe ceremonies because they're life changing and meaningful.

The Sun Dance, which is very old and sacred to the Lakota, is a traditional ceremony of personal sacrifice and prayers to help people, animals, the earth, and all things. The Sun Dancers dance for four days without food or water. Their commitment is to the great prayer to the sun, the one who gives life to all things. At the beginning and end of each session, the dancers yell "*Mitakuye oyasin,*" which is Lakota for "All my relations," dedicating their prayer to all forms of life.

Getting involved in the Sun Dance at this time in my life has been powerful for me. It has helped me rededicate myself to what's important. It has also given me a new part of myself that was never before seen. This is what the Native Americans mean when they say that each stage of life has a teaching.

When I am in the ceremony I am timeless. This is how we need to think of ourselves, as timeless. The Navajo have a prayer, "May You Walk in Beauty." This is how we should think of ourselves in terms of beauty and dignity. We can always be learning, always be creative, and always be spiritual. *Á aho! Mitakuye oyasin!*

Success

Once we begin to accept our place in the world of the thonged ones, we can focus on some of the other things that make us special. As we've mentioned before, looking at our accomplishments helps us get perspective. Sometimes, only in retrospect can we see our success. But first you must get in tune with your own personal definition of success. It's different for everyone. If you see only financial wealth as true success, then you are depriving yourself of the great satisfaction you deserve. Begin right now to create a new perspective on prosperity and abundance.

Finish this statement: Success means . . .

____

____

____

____

____

____

It's common to compare ourselves with others, although all too often we come up short. Then there are those who frequently feel a little superior. The middle ground, which is the balanced way of viewing yourself, is the one that brings the most satisfaction (even though it is rather fun to hint to your friends about how lame so many others are compared to you). This middle ground is about keeping a sense of who you are and how you compare, then concluding that you are "happy to be the way you are." Getting in that frame of mind takes effort and practice.

A short while ago, Nancy was about to attend her first Gymboree class with her baby boy. She was the only older mom signed up for this particular class, and as she sat in a suburban parking lot watching the twenty-somethings and their babies walk in, she began contemplating their differences.

> While most of these young moms are still on birth-control pills, I take hormone therapy for my perimenopause, as well as Vioxx for my osteoarthritis and Paxil for my generalized anxiety disorder.
>
> While some of them married their high school boyfriends and live ten miles from where they grew up, I'm a world-weary, twice-married, reformed obsessive-compulsive workaholic.
>
> And though I wake up in the middle of the night with hot flashes when he wakes up crying for his bottle, and my arthritic joints sometimes ache from lugging car seats and strollers, I'm not sorry for a minute that I'm an older mom. There is no way I was ready for the most important job I'll ever have—raising my son—when I was in my twenties. None of us ever know how our children will turn out, but hopefully now I have the wisdom of forty-seven years to guide me to making the right decisions.

ACTIVITY: What Makes You Different?

Ask three different people what, in their opinion, is unique about you. Hold off making any value judgment about their answers; just thank them. Once you've gotten your responses, write them in your journal. Now analyze them. Look at each response from the point of view of the person who said it. Try to see yourself through their eyes. If you find yourself turning the response into a negative one, stop and find a way to write about it in a positive way. As a recap, name three things that make you different from anyone else.

~

Cheryl is a forty-eight-year-old who has spent the last twenty years as a psychotherapist in private practice. She tells of how a trip to Bavaria changed her perspective.

IT'S ALL ABOUT WHO YOU HANG OUT WITH

Six years ago a friend of mine proposed what I then believed to be a wacky trip to Bavaria. But geography was not the reason her suggestion was exotic; we were to go to a clinic that offered injections of—are you ready?—lamb fetus cells.

Apparently, in Europe this treatment has been as basic and ordinary as a booster shot for decades—it's a respected procedure favored by celebrities and dignitaries, who regard it as a youth serum. For me, it was intriguingly bizarre with an unexpected outcome.

The night before we left, a friend who'd heard about my incipient journey called, uncharacteristically animated. She cautioned me, saying that she'd gone to a similar place in Switzerland and, immediately following the treatment, had suffered a seemingly endless bout of gray goo oozing from her pores. Ultimately, she'd passed out at the Zurich airport while waiting to board the plane home.

I was relieved to find that what awaited me was a legitimate clinic of pristine and meticulous cleanliness—something only the

Germans or my mother could produce. After an impressively professional discussion with me, the chief doctor of the clinic promised that there would be no gray goo, so I decided to go for it! (Note: No lambs are killed in this process.)

I have just come back from my third trip to Bavaria. But here's the real youth serum: Each time I go, I'm always the youngest woman there. The average age seems to hover between the mid-seventies and mid-eighties, so I've been told that I am the energy spark of the group. This perception alone, the reflection of me as young, is totally energizing. Ironically, in my own way I have found my fountain of youth—not necessarily in the cells of a lamb, but in the company I keep when I'm at the clinic.

This sense of feeling young is too easy to question outside this exquisite Bavarian scenario, with its unique choreography and casting. I find that my time surrounded by such a scintillating assortment of human characters serves to remind me to stop comparing myself with the perfect size-four, collagenated, Botoxed, lipoed, silicone-inserted babes I see in the movies—and instead look at how I fit in with the rest to the world.

Creative Visualization: New Glasses

(NUMBER SIX ON CD)

The following visualization will help you become open to looking at your life with "new eyes" and prompt you to appreciate who you are today.

Get into a comfortable position, either sitting in a chair, cross-legged on the floor, or lying down. Close your eyes. Begin to inhale through your nostrils and exhale through your mouth, gradually intensifying the deepness of your breath. With each inhalation, expand your stomach and chest, filling your lungs with air, and with each exhalation, empty your breath from your chest and stomach until they feel "collapsed." Do this very slowly. Breathe in through your nose to the count of four, hold your breath to the count of seven, then slowly exhale from your mouth to the count of eight.

With each new breath imagine yourself pulling in positive energy and everything you need, and with each exhalation feel yourself letting go of negativity and everything you don't need in your life. Do this several times.

Imagine that you are walking down a long corridor. It's wide, has an open feeling, a soft, plushy carpet, and is lined with several beautiful doors. Each door is marked with a year from a different decade, starting with the year you were born. You are comfortably walking slowly up and down the hall. The carpet is soft and cozy beneath your feet. Each door is unique and warm and inviting. When you're comfortable, go to a door and stop. Put your hand on the knob. Notice what "year" is written on the front of the door. Take a deep breath, smile, and open it.

You see an empty, cushy chair with a coffee table next to it. Sit in the chair. Get comfortable. On the little table is a pair of rose-colored glasses. As you put on the glasses, smile and ask if you can please see memories of this particular year from a new perspective. Wait there a minute, breathe, relax, and something will happen. Anything can happen and nothing can happen—it's all perfect. Now lean out and look around behind the chair. There on the floor is a present wrapped in beautiful paper with silk ribbons on it. The present is for you. You can open it now or save it for later, if you wish. If you open it now, notice what's in the box. Take a good look; then you can either keep it with you or leave it in the room. If you want to open your present later, ask if you can have it in a dream within the next few days. When you're ready, go out the door and back into the hallway.

In a moment you are going to come back to the present, feeling relaxed and refreshed. Begin by taking three deep breaths. Notice the outside sounds. Start to wiggle your fingertips and your toes. Breathing regularly, open your eyes.

Share

Be sure to process this visualization with your group or a friend or write about it in a journal. What year did you visit? What memory came up? What was in the box?

We invite you to look at your life with a new perspective. When you decide to create this turning point, you will acquire a key that will provide you with a strong sense of self-respect and the pride that comes with it. Midlife is a great time for women to own up to who they really are. It's a time to acknowledge our authentic selves and recognize how the accumulated wisdom of decades has made us perfect—just the way we are. Looking at the trials, tests, and tragedies we have lived through with a new perspective can empower us to help other women cope with the same experiences. And for some of us, it will lead us to our true calling.

Chapter Six

Turning Point No. 6: Find a New Passion

YOUR MOTHER'S MIDLIFE: *Passion? Wasn't that something she had for a few months after she got married? In midlife, it was certainly in short supply. That's not to say there weren't a few women of that generation who lived life to its fullest and then found passion in midlife, to boot. Sadly, only a small group modeled passion for something outside of the home.*

YOUR MIDLIFE: *There is a platter of rich, tempting, stimulating lifestyle choices waiting for us to try. Age no longer has to be the determining factor while we're making our midlife changes. We can find a new passion or rediscover an old one—and keep the fire burning by sharing it with others.*

Chapters 6 through 9—"Find a New Passion," "Don't Just Vent . . . Reinvent," "Make New Goals," and "Get a Coach"—are interrelated and support one overall thought: It's time to find out what you want to do next and put it into action.

A midlife goddess is full of passion. Not the lusty, sexual kind of passion (well, sometimes that, too) but passion for something that takes her to new limits. Discovering a new passion or rekindling an old one will take the "crisis" right out of your midlife. And by the way, there's nothing more sexy than a passionate woman! That's what makes her a fulfilled woman.

If you're thinking, "I have no clue what my so-called passion is beside eating rich, fattening food and spending excessive amounts of money on knickknacks," have no fear. We've provided exercises that will guide you into discovering the untapped creative part of you. But first, let's take a look at your dreams and what might have gotten between you and them.

Feeling Robbed?

Life doesn't always turn out as we dreamed it would. When we were little girls, some of the more financially fortunate ones ran around with the mistaken notion that the world revolved around them. Some of us thought that when we grew up we'd still be viewed as special. We fantasized about becoming a beautiful ballerina, a singer, an artist, a doctor, a poet, a basketball player, an interior designer—any glamorous profession. Perhaps some of us began to pursue that fantasy for a while. Then reality interrupted what was supposed to be a free and wonderful existence of fulfillment and adoration.

Some people blame others for robbing us of our turn at creative happiness. Maybe it was a parent, a sibling, or a teacher who told you you couldn't have your dream. Later on it might have been a husband, a lifestyle, a job, the economy, or too many kids that held you back. Resentment comes in imperceptible stages. What might first appear as a longing eventually shifts as the window of opportunity begins to narrow. With each passing year, we may be unaware of the stream of emotions that take hold, but we do give in to them. Anxiousness morphs into hurt, then anger, then bitterness. The good news is: You can change it now. It's today, you're forty-something, and you can let go of whatever *used to* stop you from obtaining creative enjoyment.

Did You Give Up?

Many women gave up a long time ago. Maybe creativity and self-expression were of no importance in your house. Perhaps what potential you were born with was pushed away by circumstances, and your experience was about simply surviving. Maybe you have no idea what kind of inspiration lies inside you and you simply write it off by saying, "I don't have a creative bone in my body!" or "I can't."

Perspective

Life gives us what it does. It's different for every individual. Sure, some have had it much easier than you did, but there are also others who have experienced great loss, poverty, loneliness, abuse, and neglect. Every person's background is as distinct as the next. There is no changing what has already come your way thus far. In order to realize your passion, you must take responsibility for the choices you have made up to this point. That means letting go of blaming others for the fact that you haven't pursued your dreams. It also means that you must stop blaming situations, such as not having enough money, being raised by oppressive parents, or having children before you were ready. *Stop whining and blaming!* Stop feeling sorry for yourself. Put the past in the past and go on from here. We can't ask it strongly enough: Now that you're in the middle of your life, would you like another shot a creative fulfillment? If you thought it was too late, now's the chance to change your mind.

Starting something new comes with a few risks and many bonuses. Here are some of the bonuses: new friends, a possible mentor, sharing with others, becoming a mentor, losing yourself in the fun, a broader awareness, stimulating thoughts and conversations, newly found confidence, a fresh you. Some of the risks are that certain individuals might criticize you, jealousies may arise, the new activity may cost a little money, and it might take time away from your spouse—or even your favorite television show! By now we all know that the biggest risk is not taking one.

Five Steps to a New Passion

Step 1: Discard the Old Stuff

There's a good chance we've outgrown some of our girlhood fantasies—and that's fine. Face it: Some dreams are truly "over" for us. If you still think you are going to be an astronaut, get a grip. Or if you're like Marilyn, a rejected cheerleader, you may find that once you're fifty, you no longer have the limber, lightweight body to flip-flop in front of a group of people—nor does anyone want to see her do that.

It's time to put these passé dreams to rest. The following activities will help you to separate the old wishes from the ones you'd still like to pursue.

ACTIVITY: Outgrown Your Dream?

On the lines below list at least three fantasies you had as a child that you no longer have any desire to pursue. Next to each one write a brief explanation about why you are no longer interested in it. (Note: There's a big difference between no longer holding an interest for an outdated fantasy and deciding you can't fulfill a current desire.) This list is just for the outgrown fantasies.

1. ____

____

2. ____

____

3. ____

____

Step 2: What's Behind Your Daydreams?

Now it's time to look at some hidden creative desires. Give yourself permission to explore. This is just an exercise. We're not asking you to make any kind of commitment yet, so let yourself dream.

Think: In your daydreams, are there any recurring fantasies you have of yourself? Perhaps involving a different career or an old hobby or pastime? When you see the lifestyle of someone you admire, do you wish you could do that, too? Did you ever want to become a teacher, play the piano, skydive, write poetry, or belly dance? Without judgment or even the thought of incorporating anything new into your lifestyle, make a list of whatever unrealized desires comes to mind.

____

____

____

____

____

Those were your first few thoughts. Now let yourself go. Come on, there's more to you than just those few! Dig a little deeper. See what's under there.

____

____

____

____

____

____

Step 3: What's Stopping You?

Let go of any existing definitions you have of yourself. Often we carry around all the old "should"s and "can't"s from our past. Sometimes our dreams are difficult to pursue because life's obstacles get in our way, but often we make it even more difficult by surrounding ourselves with negative people and putting ourselves in situations that prevent us from achieving our goals. It's hard enough to go after what you want in a supportive environment, let alone an adverse one. So why do we do this? Fear of what we'll find when we get there is one factor, and believing that we don't really deserve it is another.

~

"Great" people aren't always what you think they are. Most have just as many flaws as you do. Some of the great gurus are no different than your irritating neighbor. The truth is that we have a perception of how "they" live, and we put well-known people on a pedestal. It's all in your perception.

When Marilyn went from being a housewife in a little town in northern California to starring in her own NBC sitcom, she felt completely out of place. She was so thoroughly convinced that her being on a national network was all an accident that she had to find some inner strength just to play in that arena. It also helped that her neighbor was going through the same thing with her.

IT'S ALL THE SAME

I was intimidated because I was just a small-town girl who created school plays and forced her children to be in them. I had to brace myself because I knew I was going to be working with big, important television producers and other smart, creative people. This was the real thing—this was show business. To my surprise, I came to find out that the people in Hollywood and the people in the PTA were the same—only the Hollywood group dressed a lot better. That's it. Same ratio of geniuses to idiots, same competitive back stabbing, same amount of bad ideas. How disappointing. I've come to discover that it's like that in all situations—which makes me a little afraid of our political friends on Capitol Hill. There's no magical, gifted, self-assured group of nobility who are much better than you.

Woody Allen once said, "Take a good look at the movie industry. There are a handful of geniuses touched by the gods. The rest of them—if they can do it, you can do it—and you can do it better." It's only our limited experience that keeps us from seeing how the real world works.

ACTIVITY: What Would People Say?

Think of a dream you have for yourself and then complete these three sentences:

1. I'm just too ____________ to be a [your dream]______________.
2. If I tried to become a [your dream]______________, my family would______________.
3. I'm afraid that once I became a [your dream]______________, I would eventually ______________.

Those statements speak to our fear of being criticized. People are quick to nay-say when there's a little jealousy going on, or if they feel that their position is threatened. Create an environment in which you can feel supported. Come right out and ask you friends and family to support your new effort to find your unexplored passion. Here's an example of what you can say to those who make you feel intimidated:

> "I'm looking for something new in my life, and I thought I'd try ______________, but I'm feeling nervous about starting it. In the past I guess I let my fear of what you'll think or say stop me. I know that's just a silly fear I have, so I'm asking if you'd please support me in this."

What do you have to lose by saying this? That they may still laugh at you? They would have anyway. That they'll talk about you behind your back? They'll do that anyway. That they'll continue to put you down? Well, at least you tried to illicit their support. Go do it anyway! And on the other hand, they may be touched by your honesty.

ACTIVITY: Clearing Out the Clutter

The next step is to clear out the clutter. We're going to ask you to be brutal here—anything you don't truly need has to go. Think of the people in your life (friends, family, coworkers, neighbors, etc.) who you believe are nonsupportive of your efforts to try something new. Spiro Agnew called them the "nattering nabobs of negativism." If you feel that some of these people have absolutely no reason to be in your life, or in fact are a detriment to your life, get rid of them, *now*. Marilyn calls it "paring down." You don't have to have a big conversation about it with those who keep you from being your authentic self. Just ease away from those who live in the negative and make time for the people in your life who support you.

On a piece of paper create two columns. At the top of column number one write "Supportive, helpful friends." (You know where we're going with this, don't you?) At the top of column number two write "Negative, nonsupportive friends." Now list all the people you see on a regular basis—putting their names in the appropriate columns. We hope column number one is much longer than number two!

Call the number ones, go to lunch with them, e-mail them, develop an even closer relationship with them. Pick one and tell them that you are starting something new and need their support in doing it. Perhaps you could ask them to be your coach in this new endeavor. The point here is not just to glom on to people who make you feel good about yourself, but to actively ask for their support in trying something new.

Now for the number twos: first, take a minute and see if you can learn anything about yourself from the twos. Often we dislike another person because we see in them parts of ourselves we dislike. Usually it's an exaggerated version of our own negative aspect, but nonetheless it's a part of us. For example: Does this person have to be "right" all the time? Where in your life do you always have to be right? Is he or she grouchy? When are you grouchy? Does this person make snide remarks? Do you? Those are only three examples, but the point is that if you can see yourself reflected in their negative ways, you get the chance to change *you*.

Next, do your best to get rid of the number twos. Avoid them, keep any interaction to a pleasant, shallow minimum, turn down invitations to be near them. In some cases you may not be able to entirely stay clear of the number twos, but you don't have to let yourself be sucked into their pessimistic vortex.

Step 4: Baby Steps

Begin right now by choosing one activity from your list of dreams. It doesn't matter if it's the first item you wrote down or the last one. Just pick anything. Next, grab that phone book and find out where you can get instruction to learn about your new passion. Okay, it's not exactly a passion—*yet*. You are only in the exploration stage. Just make a commitment to try. Pick up that phone right now and sign up. If you want, grab a few supportive friends and do it together. Maybe your whole Fearless Aging Club will try something new together. The point is to make a commitment to something that will eventually give you abundant amounts of pleasure. You will never know unless you try.

ACTIVITY: The Perfect Day

Write a descriptive paragraph on what would be an ideal day for you. Write it in the present tense; for example: "I wake up in a great mood with lots of energy. While I'm getting dressed I notice that my clothes are slightly looser than yesterday. This makes me joyful. Breakfast is extremely healthful and delicious, and exactly what I want. I take my time eating it on the deck, where the sun is shining, the birds are singing, and there's not a leaf blower in earshot. I can't wait to go to work because I'm finally doing something I really love." And continue on, right up until bedtime.

When you've finished describing your ideal day, write these powerful words at the bottom of the page: *This or something better is manifesting itself for the good of all concerned.*

Step 5: Share It

Once you've discovered something new you can feel passionate about, share your enthusiasm with others. Marilyn writes about an experience she and Nancy shared not only with each other but also with many women.

THE COLONY

One evening Nancy and I had dinner together and talked about stress, Prozac, sex, therapy, kids, getting old, and art. Yes, art. Nancy had just painted with some acrylics on a piece of sketch paper and was intrigued by how good it had felt to accomplish one little, "sort-of" painting. Like most of us, Nancy had dabbled in art when she was in junior high, but she'd left "real art" to the "talented ones." I'd been slightly more active in the sport, but I'd leaned toward the crafts portion of arts and crafts. That night, we just up and decided to try our hand at, of all things, oil painting.

Then we brought this idea to our friend Caryl. She exclaimed that she needed to fill some huge, empty walls in her house. So without a second thought or any training, we cleared out Caryl's garage, hung a drape in one corner, placed a wooden bowl of lemons and blood oranges in front of it, slipped on some smocks and berets, and began our first oil paintings ever. We knew right away that we had found a new passion. What we didn't yet know was how this passion would change our lives.

We started meeting every Monday. Our enthusiasm was contagious. Other women joined what was now called the Art Colony. We hired my fourteen-year-old daughter, an art student of five years, to teach us the fundamentals. With lots of encouragement from our families, the six of us, aged forty to fifty-two, inexperienced as a newborn, started producing beautiful works of art. No kidding.

We found that as a result of this experience other parts of our lives began to flow more freely. We no longer spent the better part of the night worrying about the pressures of work, the lack of it, the kids' grades, getting old, or taxes, but instead fantasized about our next painting.

Whenever we would meet and paint, it would remind me of my grandmother's quilting bee. As women do so well, we would open up while working on our projects, and the advice, gossip, inspiration, and laughter would flow like the colors we were blending on our canvases. (Okay, so some of that creativity makes me get carried away.) We were learning about much more than art, though; we were experiencing a revitalization of the soul.

Nine months later we had produced more than ten fabulous works of art each, so we decided it was time for a gallery show. Nobody told us that the art world was elite and snobbish, so we just went about the business of creating a grand opening in a gallery in the Los Angeles arts district. About a hundred people showed up, and more than a few were in shock over how prolific we were, but even more couldn't get over the fact that these novice women had actually gotten their "outsider artwork" into a gallery. Later we discovered that an artist has to be "juried" by gallery owners and most people who show in a gallery are already quite established in the art world. It's a good thing we didn't know that, or we might have been too intimidated to try it.

Whether it's oil painting, ceramics, teaching, ice skating, volunteering, tap dancing, scouting garage sales, or horseback riding, when you put something new in your life and share it with others, it can set you up for passion and joy that can sustain you for many years to come. And sharing it only intensifies the happiness.

QUESTION

Other than money, what is the first thing that comes to mind when asked why you aren't pursuing your passion?

The Story of Ana

For those of you that think the deck is stacked against you, that you are too busy, too old, too poor, not talented enough, not smart enough, not brave enough, not whatever enough, we have a story for you. It's the story of Ana, who worked part-time for Marilyn as her housekeeper. Marilyn explains:

Ana came to this country eleven years ago from El Salvador, where she'd lived in poverty. When she was six years old, unfortunate circumstances demanded that she and her five siblings separate from their mother and live with an abusive, cruel grandmother. Ana, the oldest, was always told that she was wrong, a bad child, and good for nothing, and she was beaten for any small mistake. At sixteen she left her grandmother's brutal dominance and, with her mother, began cleaning houses in another town. When she was thirty she found her way to this country. She is currently raising three children, as well as her two grandchildren, while working as a domestic for three families.

On the days she worked at my house she would see me tackling one kind of art project or another. When the Art Colony met, Ana would often observe five or six women intensely painting in oils. Little did we know how she longed to try it herself.

In the spirit of sharing our newly found passion, Nancy and I began to host art retreats. For the weekend of the first retreat, we had hired Ana to help prepare meals and clean. As we began some of the activities, we realized that it was uncomfortable to be "empowering women" when the one who needed the most empowerment was cleaning up after us. It became perfectly clear that though we needed her help, she needed to join the group.

For the first night's activity we had asked each woman to bring a symbol that represented the carefree, passionate days of her girlhood. As they began to show us their symbols and share their stories, we felt touched, seeing adult women become transformed by the memories of those days of freedom and innocence. A model horse prompted images of a band of gangly preteens jumping over suburban hedges as they pretended to be a herd of wild mustangs. A tiny ceramic statue of a little girl in a tutu brought back the wide-eyed joy and wonder of a first dance recital. A tangerine was a reminder of a summer playing in the orchards with wild cousins.

Then it was time for Ana to share. She told us it was difficult for her to find a symbol to represent joy and freedom, because her childhood had been anything but carefree. At age five, Ana was locked in the house and left alone to care for her two infant siblings while her mother cleaned houses in order to feed her family. But Ana recalled one happy memory. She pulled out her symbol, which she had gotten from the kitchen—a frying pan and some rice grains. She stirred the uncooked rice as she told us this story:

> "I had been watching my mother fix the rice for the dinner each night, so one night I wanted to surprise her. After she had gone to work, I took the stool and got the rice off a high shelf and the matches and some beans. I did everything my mommy would do to make the dinner, so that when she came home, the dinner would be all ready for her. I didn't really know what I was doing, I was only five—so I just did what I could remember. I didn't know that you were supposed to put water in with the rice. When my mommy saw me, she was so happy that I'd tried. Right then she started over and taught me how to do it the right way. I remember being so happy that I'd helped my mother."

We were touched by her story and felt humbled (and a little spoiled). Ana's symbol involved a memory of doing something for someone else, because that's one of the few things that had brought her happiness. At forty-two years of age, Ana still had never taken the time to do anything for herself. Up until that weekend her only passion had been "survival" for herself and her children, and the comfort of her religion. There wasn't time in her life for indulgences. She told us how she had been watching us paint, that she was drawn to the bright colors of the oil paintings she had seen at the Colony, but that she didn't think she could ever do anything like that.

The next day Ana painted for ten straight hours. She intensely examined the still life we had set up and put the image on canvas the way she saw it. The other women would come by her painting and cry out, "Ana! That's beautiful!" Ana began to glow. She left that weekend retreat with a still life any artist would be proud of. Now a full-time member of the Colony, Ana is producing vividly hued canvases of her native San Salvador, reminiscent of the style of Cézanne. She was the first of us to sell a painting.

Ana could have said, "I'm too old, too uneducated, too poor, too busy, too scared to try something new in my life." But instead she picked up a paintbrush and opened the door to a whole new world.

Recently she was in an art-supply store replenishing some of her oil paints when the clerk, assuming that she was buying them for her "boss," asked if she was sure those were the exact colors her employer wanted. Ana smiled as she said, "Ah no, these are for me. I am the artist!"

ACTIVITY: The Girl Within

The activity we did that night is called Finding the Girl Within. It's about looking into the past to recapture the sense of wonder and aliveness that came so naturally to us as children. Try this activity for your next meeting:

For homework, each member of the group should remember a period in her life when she was a young girl, perhaps between the ages of nine and twelve. Try to capture a time when you were playful, wild, perhaps a little full of yourself. Be sure it includes some form of laughter and a sense of freedom.

If you need to, you can help prompt these memories by going back through old photo albums, or maybe you even have a box of letters or postcards. (Remember camp?) Pick one memory and then find a symbol that represents that memory.

When you next meet with your group, one at a time show your symbol and talk in detail about this incident. Include feelings, colors, smells, and sounds. Remember how confident and alive you felt? What happened to that sense of magic, of endless possibilities in our lives?

Then ask each woman to think of times in her adult life when she had this same sense of wonder and excitement. (And don't include any drug- or alcohol-induced happiness.) What were they? Where did they take place and what activity were you doing?

What similarities come up? Do you notice any patterns taking hold? What do you need to do to feel that much "alive" again?

Creative Visualization: Try Something New

(NUMBER SEVEN ON CD)

This particular visualization will give you a chance to experience four new activities within the realm of your glorious imagination. There will be no one there to judge you, so feel free to really express yourself.

Get into a comfortable position, either sitting in a chair, cross-legged on the floor, or lying down. Close your eyes. Begin to inhale through your nostrils and exhale through your mouth, gradually intensifying the deepness of your breath. With each inhalation, expand your stomach and chest, filling your lungs with air, and with each exhalation, empty your breath from your chest and stomach until they feel "collapsed." Do this very slowly. Breathe in through your nose to the count of four, hold your breath to the count of seven, then slowly exhale from your mouth to the count of eight. With each new breath imagine yourself pulling in positive energy and everything you need, and with each exhalation feel yourself letting go of negativity and everything you don't need in your life. Do this several times.

Imagine for a few minutes that you are ready to learn to paint in oils. You enter a private studio and see a big, empty, white canvas. Because this is your imagination, you can view that canvas as alluring, calling your name, rather than as intimidating. A wise and supportive teaching guide is waiting to show you how to begin. You spread the colorful oils onto your palette and smell their rich scent. It's all good and warm and inviting. Your teaching guide explains to you that you have your own, individual self-expression, which will come out as you paint. So, with a little excitement, you put one color after another on the canvas.

Now imagine it's three months later. You've found your own particular style and you are brimming with ideas. You can't wait to get started. In the past few months you have discovered that certain individuals are attracted to, and greatly appreciate, your style—while others don't get it. Neither has any affect on you because the very process—from idea to finished product—is so pleasant and stimulating to you. You are happy that you gave yourself the courage to try something new.

Next, it's your first day to go skydiving. Remembering that this is all in your imagination, you set yourself up for having the time of your life. Your teaching guide shows you all the gear you need and helps you get into it. You smile as you step into the plane. As you are ascending you just know this is going to be fun and thrilling. The pilot tells you that you will be perfectly safe because you are with the best instructor in the world. You understand that this jump is a tandem one with your teaching guide. Strapped to your instructor, you feel ready and safe as you both take that first leap. As you are free-falling, you are aware that this jump represents many new things you will try now that you are in the middle of your life. The jump is the perfect symbol for the courage and bravery you truly hold within yourself. It's breathtaking and beautiful. You land softly and feel proud of yourself.

Imagine that it's three months later. You've jumped more than fifty times and you know exactly what to do. You can't wait to get started. You appreciate everything about this newfound pleasure—from suiting up to psyching up. You are grateful that you had the courage to try something new.

Because this is still your imagination, you get to try something else. See yourself sitting at a computer typing away. You are a writer. You're clever, unique, and talented—something you've only recently discovered. You have your own, individual self-expression, which grows stronger the more you write. So, with anticipation you begin telling a story about a significant time in your life. As you let your story flow onto the page, you realize how cathartic it is. You love letting it all out. You have a great knack for telling the truth and for self-editing, as well. You had no idea of this talent of yours until you tried. Now you don't want to stop. So instead of looking forward to more television shows, you find yourself stimulated by your own stories.

Next, you get to choose a fourth activity to try. Make it something you've always wondered about. Are you a singer? A ballet dancer or a belly dancer? Are you a motivational speaker, a teacher, a comedian? Maybe you are dancing with the Native American Indians, or playing basketball with other women. Maybe you're teaching children a craft or an English lesson. Whatever it is, it's fun and stimulating to you. Stay with this picture of yourself and pretend you've been doing it for quite a while. Imagine yourself confident in your actions, happy to be doing what has become your new passion. Take some time here to really picture this.

You know that there is a creative activity that's right for you. And you also know that you can make it fun and exciting just by taking that first step. Give yourself permission to begin a new chapter in your life—one that fulfills your imaginative nature.

In a moment you are going to come back to the present, feeling relaxed and refreshed. Begin by taking three deep breaths. Notice the outside sounds. Start to wiggle your fingertips and your toes. Breathing regularly, open your eyes.

Share

Don't forget to process this visualization with your group or a friend or write about it in a journal. What was the fourth activity for you? When are you going to make that first call?

~

Have you ever heard this quote: "Most of us go to our grave with our music still inside of us"? You don't want that to be you. As you realize that this chapter could be another important turning point for you, you can start seeking activities that will soothe your soul. There are many—not just one—that can give you a sense of passion for something new. And that sense of passion is what will draw other creative people to you. You will have the look of a happy woman. Now is the best time to begin. Don't wait another minute. Become the fulfilled woman you deserve to be.

Chapter Seven

Turning Point No. 7: Don't Just Vent . . . Reinvent

YOUR MOTHER'S MIDLIFE: *Reinvention was something that happened to her, not something she did herself. Why risk rocking the boat of stability?*

YOUR MIDLIFE: *Shake it up! Today, women are giving themselves permission to change their lives in major ways—they know it's not too late!*

Reinventing oneself means lovingly and respectfully letting go of who you were before this moment and embracing a new you. Reinvention also means taking some big risks. This is the ideal time (the middle of your life) to take the risk to become well-rounded, fascinating, stimulated, and happy.

Read some of fifty-four-year-old Suzy's thoughts about reinventing yourself and see if you can let her lead you toward a new attitude.

"WHAT TO DO? WHAT TO DO?"

Change spreads its legs when you become fifty-plus . . . the air is rife with options. And for the first time in your life, you don't give a damn about things that were vital to you just a few short years ago. It's startling, because you have to ask yourself what you *do* care about. And once you discover an answer, Hamlet's problem confounds you—namely, "What to do? What to do?"

Sometimes "What to do?" is solved by realizing what you give a damn about. That's a big step, and it may cause your friends and family some pain. But it is the wise goddess who can welcome change. One is given only a finite number of opportunities, but this amount skyrockets when you pitch in and give an opportunity the chance to refocus your life.

One of the legacies of being an American is the possibility for reinvention. Madonna does it every other Tuesday, for God's sake.

Sometimes you have to learn a new skill before you can take the plunge. Consider computers: New and endless possibilities await us if we open up. I love the computer I'm writing this on. It has put such a challenge in my life. My son-in-law is Horowitz on the laptop; I can't help myself from groveling in his presence. (Oh, we are unworthy! I pray for the day when he asks me what's the difference between a delphinium and a hydrangea. Now, *that* would be a great day!) At any rate, it is disconcerting to realize that you know nothing about something that schoolchildren take for granted. So take a class, already. Three months or so of homework and you've got it!

The stimulation—on both the stress side and the fulfilling side—of learning something new and then becoming passionate about it far outweighs the risks that come with reinventing oneself. You're only "sort of young" once—let yourself play!

Reinvention begins with looking at what has now become your priorities. Over the years they have shifted here and there. Try this exercise for the next few weeks and see what seeps out.

ACTIVITY: Dig a Little Deeper

An old and powerful technique (that a lot of us tend to resist) can bring out the creative side of our subconscious, further solidify our goals, and help us become aware of the negative messages we might be holding on to. The old, tried, and true exercise is to write in a journal, daily. Julia Cameron, author of the best-selling book *The Artist's Way,* recommends what she calls "morning pages." She describes them as three pages of longhand writing, strictly stream-of-consciousness meanderings, the purpose being that we can drain out all the angry, whiny, petty stuff on paper, leaving room for the creative stuff.

To help you get in touch with what you truly want to accomplish in the next years, we recommend that you do at least a three-week journal dedicated to exploring your empty areas and looking into what you are authentically drawn to. Take this exercise seriously. Write in your journal every morning. Do it when you first wake up; that way you'll be fresh and won't be carrying the irritations of the day with you. Set your alarm early if you have to. Begin by writing about anything that comes to mind. The more petty the writing, the more junk you'll be releasing. Don't judge what you're writing. Don't even look back at it for the first week. Just let it all out. Soon you'll find some of the stumbling blocks that have been keeping you from realizing your potential. Creative ideas for your future will reveal themselves in the pages of your journal. Self-discovery takes discipline. Even if you just do your journaling for the few weeks it takes you to finish reading this book, it will give you incredible perspective and some marvelous ideas.

Priorities of the Heart

We recommend ending each journal entry with a "priority list," not to be confused with a "to do" list of such things as picking up groceries. This priority list concentrates on the most important aspects of your life as you see it. Each day, before you get sidetracked with the minutiae of daily living, remind yourself of your "Priorities of the Heart." Ask yourself, "What are the most important goals I want to achieve for the rest of my life?" Is it to have better relationships with family and loved ones? The pursuit of a passion? The realization of a dream? Acceptance of your authentic self? All of the above? Every day spent on establishing these priorities, every moment lived with an awareness of what you truly hope to accomplish in this life, will eventually result in a more fulfilled existence.

~

Sometimes we let ourselves get to the point of total frustration or burn out before we muster up the courage to do the work of reinventing ourselves. This next story, from fifty-nine-year-old Lilka, demonstrates some of the feelings a lot of us experience before we move into action.

FROM SCHOOLTEACHER TO SEXOLOGIST?

After marrying, in my early thirties, and starting my family, I longed to be home with my babies. I had studied to be a teacher, so I felt quite comfortable starting a play school for one-and-a-half to three-year-olds.

Six years later, when I had done everything I could do with this age group, I picked up the newspaper one day and discovered a job in a student-exchange program. Running a student-exchange program had been my lifelong dream. For twelve years I'd worked in this field. My husband and I eventually started our own organization, called Cultural Homestay International. By this time, I was forty years old. In the initial years, the creative process exhilarated us, although we had to cope with the enormous strain of starting a new business. Three years later, I found I had become restless; the exchange organization, which had grown so big, seemed to have less room for creativity every day.

I began to search for something personal to do with my life that would still be as meaningful. The years were flying by. We noticed that our two girls, one nine and the other twelve, were growing up, and we envisioned an empty nest too soon. At this point, we decided to have our last baby.

After the "late in life" baby was born, I was constantly torn between the two forces of running a business and taking care of the baby. In fact, I was growing ever more stressed and angry. My husband, showing few signs of stress, did not seem to mind traveling all over the country and the world, promoting and selling our organization. In fact, he was totally fulfilled. I, on the other hand, felt great reluctance and some guilt about constantly leaving home. I had put Michelle in a morning play school for toddlers, but I never seemed to have enough time for myself; nor did I have any time for fun. I began to harbor secret plans of going back to school.

One night, my husband bounced into the house, grabbed the two older children, and went blithely off to the movies. I was left alone with the baby (my job). My rage overflowed. I did not have anyone to vent to. I decided to run away from home. I wanted the rest of the family to worry and fret when I wasn't there waiting to dote on them when they got home. I picked up my little three-year-old daughter and went off to the local late-night bookstore. We sat in the children's section reading books together. When I was sure everyone was back home, I slowly returned.

Of course, they'd hardly noticed that I was gone. When I walked in the door and explained that I had intended to run away but had ended up at the bookstore, they laughed and went on their merry ways. This was when I decided to reinvent. No one took any responsibility for my life. No one was going to fix my life but me. No one really cared that I was fuming, frustrated, and fatigued.

That very night, I filled out an application for the Institute for the Advanced Study of Human Sexuality. Back in school, I struggled for four years to get ready for my board exams, and for nine more to complete my dissertation on the sexuality of large women.

It seems that anger, as painful as it was and as much as I would have preferred to ignore it, was tremendously influential in propelling me forward in my life.

As we begin to take the path to something new, we often come across stumbling blocks. A big one is fear. If you've decided that you need to go back to college or a trade school, you may wrestle with doubts about fitting in and looking stupid or wonder if you'll even finish what you start. Here's a passage from fifty-year-old Bev that might help you see some of the benefits of going back to school while you are middle-aged.

BACK TO SCHOOL

Thirty-two years ago, I graduated from high school and started, but never completed, college. A age forty-nine, I went back to school. Not having taken college courses for several decades, I was anxiety ridden about attending a school where the majority of students are twenty-somethings; of rekindling my old (bad) study habits; of making a fool of myself in class discussions. I think I've been procrastinating all these years for those exact reasons.

My anxiety was assuaged when the "midlife-ripened me" emerged that first day in class. Right after the initial fish-out-of-water feeling subsided, I felt mellow and more self-assured than I ever had as a nineteen-year-old. Something about having all those years of life experience behind me provided a personal comfort factor that hadn't been present in my youth.

Without the distractions of youthful pursuits (sex) and educational goals (the ones my parents wanted for me), I'm enjoying the luxury of actually wanting to learn the subject matter. I've engaged in many class discussions—without feeling fearful of someone challenging my opinions, as I once did. I trust my own perspective and believe in my convictions. Yet I remain open to others. There was a time when I just had to have the answer. Now I'm open to hearing arguments against my points of view, and can accept incorporating some changes in my perceptions. As a younger person, the need to form strong and unyielding opinions held great importance—after all, I was trying to firmly establish my place in the world with that early, unwavering belief system. And remarkably, I now have no qualms about admitting that "I don't know."

I've tackled the reading assignments with gusto, mainly

because learning this material is something I've elected to do, and not because my graduation requirements demand that I take the course!

The importance of being "all knowing" subsides with age. Even better yet, it's replaced with the understanding that you'll never know it all—and that's a great burden lifted.

Sometimes it's our belief system that stops us from trusting that we can succeed at a new job or lifestyle. There are certain rules someone made up, and we think we can't break them. Especially when the rule says, "You're too old to do that." Marilyn didn't know about that rule when she started the comedy show *The Mommies*.

FROM HOUSEWIFE TO TV STAR: THE ACCIDENT

I was forty-two and already in the middle of my third midlife crisis when I heard a voice whispering gently in my ear, "You are no longer exciting . . . better take a class." Like most American women who have turned forty, I thought, "Wow, wouldn't it be fun to be an actress?" Then came the rules: "Wait a minute. . . . It's too late. In Hollywood women in their thirties are cast aside." I ignored that fear by telling myself, "Well, if Olympia Dukakis can do it, then I can, too." Anyway, I really just wanted to do a little community theater with other local frustrated midlifers, but before I knew it I was starring in my own sitcom on NBC.

How did I get there? Well, I just started following my heart, gambled on a few middle-aged risks, and then life took over for me.

It was 1990 when I read the ad in the paper touting acting classes for adults. I mustered up the courage to enroll, but the first night I realized it wasn't exactly what I had in mind. I sat there in a circle doing Chekhov with nineteen-year-olds. Hadn't the paper said, "for adults"? I needed to find a friend who didn't call me *dude*. And it had to be someone who could rip on the other class members with me on the ride home.

The next day I called my neighbor Caryl. I had a feeling she'd be up for a little adventure because she was starving for attention. Every time we got together out on the front lawn she would entertain the other mothers of the cul-de-sac with her rendition of the Solid Gold Dancers. She'd hump her garage, winging her hair around just like her favorite dancer, Darcel. It was obvious that she needed to release herself.

We didn't last long in the acting class, because they were thespians and we were mothers. They wanted to conquer Shakespeare; we wanted to get out of the house. So we put together this silly stage show and advertised it as "a show for women who don't want sex more than once a month." We actually called the local newspaper and got an article written about our "phenomenal stage act" before we had even written one word. Now, that's commitment! By the way, at that point I had never even seen a comedian perform live. I wasn't trying to be a comedian, anyway. I was simply having my midlife fun.

Because this arena was so new to us, we needed lots of practice and bravery. So one Thursday night just before our first show, we transformed Caryl's living room into a comedy club and had our first ever dress rehearsal. We invited twenty of our most supportive and trustworthy friends—and forced a few family members—to attend what must have been the most pitiful display of raw talent and blind courage. We never even knew their innermost thoughts because we had one rule for the audience that night: "You must encourage us. We are just too nervous to hear criticism. There will be plenty of time to rip on us later, but tonight you must tell us only what you liked about the show."

I believe that this was one of the most important elements of our success. You must surround yourself with those who will encourage you, and you must ask for encouragement. Nevertheless, I am still afraid and embarrassed that there's a video floating around somewhere of me trying to do a comedy bit about my allergies.

We set up a hundred chairs for our first real show because it was impossible to guess how many people would show up after having read the newspaper article, and we knew nothing about presale. At around seven o'clock they began to arrive. Our hearts pounded as we saw women of all ages, wearing blazers and jeans, in groups of six, getting out of their minivans. They were chatting and laughing and saving seats for friends. And there were a lot of them. Standing room only. Caryl and I looked at each other from behind the curtain and said, "Wow, there must be a lot of women who don't want sex more than once a month!"

We opened with a poorly choreographed dance number to the song "Nine to Five." We were dressed in business suits and carried briefcases with fake babies in them. Midway through the song we threw the babies into the audience. They loved it! I look back on it now and wonder just how hard up for fun these suburban women must have been to think we were entertaining. The show was two and a half hours long!

The next morning after carpool, I received an intriguing call from an audience member who had come to the show from a neighboring town. She'd gotten my phone number out of the book and was calling to give me "feedback." Our first critic told me in a very gentle way all the things she liked and didn't like about the act. I took notes. It was the beginning of the many things we learned directly from our audience. After that, we made it a policy to go straight from the stage into the crowd and listen to their comments.

Stay-at-home moms tend to think of themselves as inexperienced, but I think they already know the greater part of running a corporate business. Whenever they're nabbing someone to help with school fund-raisers, they're using selling skills. When they have meetings with the school counselor, they're negotiating. When they're getting something donated, they're closing. We just don't give these skills the powerful names they deserve, but we do it all and we do it well.

Word of mouth began with the first show, and in each new town the size of the audience grew considerably. Within six months we needed to rent small theaters that could accommodate an audience of five hundred or more. We had tapped into a market of people whose only nights out were the monthly PTA meetings and an occasional children's movie. No wonder they thought we were funny.

Driving to the show one night, I got this surge of excitement. I said, "Think about it—all because of us, six hundred women are going to have a really fun time tonight!" We were in awe.

At this juncture, we began using alternative methods to get closer to our goals. Visualizations, meditations, self-talk, therapy—we incorporated it all. In my "goal book," I began drawing pictures of situations I wanted to come true, like relaxing on stage or selling out every new venue, being featured in an article in *People* magazine, getting an agent, and landing lots of contracts.

When we examined the deeper reasons for doing the show, we came to realize that things like becoming famous and making lots of money were only fun outgrowths of the more truthful reasons for creating our show. Understanding those true reasons kept us strong and grounded. Put simply, we realized that we wanted women to feel that they were not alone. That's it. That is the truthful reason we wanted, and needed, to do the show.

The Mommies' stage show evolved over the following year and a half, and to our astonishment, before we even knew where to go next, we got offers from ABC, CBS, and NBC to star in our own sitcom. We were in shock. I still am. Especially now that our little show has come and gone. We busted a lot of rules that said, "You can't." I was forty-four when I first stepped onto that Paramount soundstage. I had never acted in so much as a school play. I didn't even watch television back then.

I believe that our success came from, first of all, being naive, and then from trusting and appreciating the process (it's still one big adventure to us). We flourished because we enjoyed the moment, took phenomenal risks, had a good, solid friendship to hold on to, were old enough to keep our priorities straight, and happened to be graced with a certain amount of luck.

Sometimes we can reinvent ourselves by going back into the working world—without going back to school or doing any major preparation. There will always be an adjustment period when you are the new kid. But often it doesn't last for long, and the uncomfortableness can be stimulating.

With both her girls in college, single mom Mary decided to look for a new job—one that took her outside of her small-town comfort zone. Mary is an innovative, reliable, conscientious, and fun fifty-two-year-old. It's fitting that she found something new and stimulating. Here's a little story about her adjustment to the world of commuting.

THE COMMUTER

So far, the job is going great. Quite a life adjustment, I'll tell you. As part of the process, I have become "BART Woman." (BART stands for Bay Area Rapid Transit—the commuter system in the San Francisco Bay area.) It was so weird at first, waiting in the BART station amid all these people calmly standing in line reading or zoning out, when to me it felt as exciting as a Disneyland ride. Well, it even looks like the monorail. On my first day, a young African-American woman across the aisle sneezed loudly three or four times, so naturally, I said "Bless you!" She totally ignored me, leading me to realize that there are certain "BART rules," as if you are supposed to exist in individual BART bubbles of individual "space," not communicating or being affected by your surroundings. I was trying to erect my own BART bubble when this executive-looking man with a briefcase got in and sat down next to me. He was also carrying a large jar of peanut butter. C'mon, how could I *not* say anything? I looked at him and quietly asked, "Your week for the peanut butter?" He replied, "Well, it comes in handy if the train gets stuck in the tunnel for six hours, like last week." I was aghast, imagining myself being six hours late for work my first week. "*What?!*" I asked in horror. He laughed. "So, BART newcomer, are you?"

Now I just look for the inner sparkle of other BART rebels, those of us who refuse to encase ourselves in the BART bubbles of existential angst. Life can be such an adventure—especially after fifty, when being uncool is just daily fare.

There's the reinvention of women like Lilka, Marilyn, and Mary, who, after years of raising kids, needed to get out of the house. And then there's the opposite kind: Many middle-aged women in today's society find themselves in a biological bind—they forgot to have kids! Joanne's story may give you support if your eggs are going bye-bye and you still want to become a mommy.

HAVING A BABY AT FIFTY

A few years ago I realized that my mother was going to die. At that moment, I decided to adopt a daughter of my own. I've always felt that the mother-daughter relationship is the deepest, most primal connection imaginable. And with my own mother moving toward the end of her life, I wanted to continue to experience this profound bond with a child of my own.

Becoming a mom at fifty was perfect for me. I'd already lived life to the fullest—you know: Been there, done that. The only thing I'd really missed was having a child. I'd always felt that it was kind of unfair that men could have children until they were seventy or eighty, but women had a biological cutoff date. Nevertheless, I didn't let my age get in the way of an intensely profound new chapter in my life. I realized that adoption provided a direct route for me to have a family of my own, and I started the process immediately. I haven't regretted my decision for one instant.

Every day my heart is filled with pure joy when my daughter runs to meet me at the door. And the time we spend together is deeply connected, powerfully in the moment, and positively euphoric.

Sure it's hard at times, exhausting and emotionally draining. And, after years of being responsible for only myself, it isn't easy to be completely responsible for another human being. The reality of being a mom can't be easily explained; the enormous depth of love one feels for a child can't be described. But it can be experienced by anyone with a true desire for it. And age and marital status are really irrelevant.

Creative Visualization: The Picture Window

(NUMBER EIGHT ON CD)

Get into a comfortable position, either sitting in a chair, cross-legged on the floor, or lying down. Close your eyes, begin to inhale through your nostrils and exhale through your mouth, gradually intensifying the deepness of your breath. With each inhalation, expand your stomach and chest, filling your lungs with air, and with each exhalation, empty your breath from your chest and stomach until they feel "collapsed." Do this very slowly. Breathe in through your nose to the count of four, hold your breath to the count of seven, then slowly exhale from your mouth to the count of eight. With each new breath imagine yourself pulling in positive energy and everything you need, and will each exhalation feel yourself letting go of negativity and everything you don't need in your life. Do this several times.

See yourself walking down a neighborhood street at dusk. It's a warm evening—very comfortable. There are beautiful trees and interesting houses. The lights are on in the homes, illuminating the activities inside them. Each house has a picture window. As you slowly walk along the street you can see clearly through the picture windows into the living rooms of each home. You see a person in each living room doing an activity that they seem to be enjoying with every inch of their being. Coincidentally, these are all activities that you also love to do. Imagine some of them. Someone might be playing the piano, lost within the music. Another might be dancing joyfully with a partner. Perhaps they are painting or sculpting a work of art with great passion. They may be tutoring a young student. They may be at a computer, writing words that only they have the power to express. You are drawn to one of these activities above all the others.

You decide to go up to their front door and ring the doorbell, so that you can meet the person inside in order to find out how they came to realize their passion. You ring the doorbell. The door opens. You look at the person, and the person is you. You ask yourself, "How did you realize this great passion?" Pay close attention to the answer. Then you ask, "How did you find the time?" The person at the door representing you answers, "It's time I took care of myself. All I had to do is begin." Hug that person that is you and thank them for the encouragement, then walk away. As you are walking down that quiet, warm street, you repeat, "It's time I took care of myself. All I have to do is begin."

In a moment you are going to come back to the present, feeling relaxed and refreshed. Begin by taking three deep breaths. Notice the outside sounds. Start to wiggle your fingertips and your toes. Breathing regularly, open your eyes.

Share

Describe what you saw in the visualization. What activity were you drawn to the most intensely? What did the person representing you reply when asked the question "How did you realize your great passion?"

QUESTION

A fairy godmother gives you the ability to do anything you want to do for the next year of your life. What do you choose to do?

So, stop waiting until you finish school . . . or until you go back to school . . . or until your finish your degree . . . or until you lose ten pounds . . . or until you have kids . . . or until your kids leave the house . . . or until you retire . . . or until you get married . . . or until you get divorced . . . or until Friday night . . . or until you get a new car or home . . . or until your car is paid off . . . or until spring . . . or until September . . . or until the first or the fifteenth . . . or until your song comes on . . . or until you've had a drink . . . or until you've sobered up . . . or until you die . . . to decide that there is no better time than *right now* to reinvent yourself.

Chapter Eight

Turning Point No. 8: Make New Goals

YOUR MOTHER'S MIDLIFE: *Most of our dear mothers didn't think about making new, life-changing goals once they turned fifty—other than planning a cruise, taking the grandkids to Disneyland, upgrading the motor home, and figuring out if they should keep their medical insurance or go with Kaiser Permanente.*

YOUR MIDLIFE: *There is a great big world out there to discover—and plenty of time left to do it. Climb Mount Everest? Go back to school? Have a baby at fifty through an egg donor? Set a goal and do it!*

With the awareness you now have, after reading this book and working on the exercises, you might suspect that when we recommend that you make new goals it's with the idea that now is the time to put your dreams into action. The way the years have been whizzing by lately, it's fitting that you get organized in order to enjoy the results before it's too late. This is not an exercise in realizing simple New Year's resolutions; these are life-altering, fulfilling aspirations. This is a critical self-induced turning point. Let's make it happen.

Making goals and keeping them are two separate accomplishments. Obviously, we'll start with creating the goals that will best serve you for the second half of your life. The following chapter, entitled "Get a Coach," will help you with the follow-through. Think of some new (or festering) goals. Goals for the forty-something or fifty-something woman are uniquely different from the goals of the years past. What do you want to be doing in five years? Ten? Think seriously about that. How old will you be in ten years? How old will your kids be? What, if any, job will you be doing? We'll take you through several activities that will help you get connected to some significant, personal future plans, and then we'll help you to accomplish them.

ACTIVITY: My Next Five Years

Answer the following questions in order to begin the process of creating something new in your life.

What will the date be five years from now? ____________________

Exactly how old will you be? _______

Will you be working? _______

At the same job? _______

Will you be retired? _______

What will you be doing to earn a living? ________________________

If you could do anything you wanted to, anything at all, what passion would you be immersed in five years from today? __________

____

What are the things you might be telling yourself these days that stop you from even trying? ____

____

What would you tell your best friend if she wanted to pursue that dream? Give her some words of encouragement.________________

____

Now say those same words to yourself.

ACTIVITY: The Five-Year Party

There's a fun activity that we originally learned from author Jack Canfield. It's called the Five-Year Party. You plan a wonderful evening where everyone invited is requested to come "as you want to be in five years." The guests arrive with props like books they will have written, trophies they will have earned, children they will have had, and big paychecks they will have received. Everyone is asked to stay in character throughout the night. They talk about their latest achievements, how happy they are now, and what they're up to next. Anything goes at this party. It's also fun to have a reunion party five years later to see how many things have come true.

Marilyn has a story about the party she and her friend Caryl put on six years ago.

> I giggle whenever I think about our Five-Year Party. Caryl and I went all out with fake paparazzi, *Entertainment Tonight* interviews, and a red-carpet entrance. I had sent telegrams to the party house from famous people congratulating everyone on their accomplishments. Caryl and I carried around copies of our new *Mommy Book*. I'd made mock books with a cover using this crazy picture of us wearing plastic flamingos on our heads—the only photo I could drum up that afternoon. At that time we didn't even have an outline, let alone a book deal.
>
> Two years later HarperCollins released our book *The Mother Load,* and by pure coincidence, out of all the head shots we submitted for the jacket, the photograph they decided to use was the same one I used on the "fake" book jacket. The book did very well—went through three hardcover printings and eventually also sold as a paperback.
>
> Nancy brought a baby doll to the party and was carrying around a self-help book she had written. Both those things have come to pass as I write this little piece.
>
> Six years ago my daughter was ten and in elementary school. Because I was afraid she'd be a horrid, naughty, sassy teenager

within the next five years, I hired a young fifteen-year-old to play my darling, loving, "good yet normal" teenage daughter. I provided her with a script. She burst into the house and kissed my cheek, exclaiming how great it was that we had this special relationship where we talked about everything and hardly ever fought. She said she couldn't stay long because she was on her way to a party with her designated driver and, while she was quite a healthy, normal teenager, I really had nothing to worry about because she never got carried away with drinking alcohol or smoking pot. I also had to throw this in: She explained that she was going to see Denzel Washington's son at the party. The whole bit got lots of laughs.

Fast-forward six years. First of all, my daughter and I have that special relationship I dreamed about. I don't know why, but we do talk about everything (okay, I'm not dumb . . . certain things are saved for best friends and siblings). We rarely ever fight, she's a wise and moderate teenager, and she actually goes to parties with Denzel's son. It's true! When I'd made up that little scenario I'd had no idea if Denzel lived here in Los Angeles or in New York; I didn't even know if he had kids. What are the chances that my daughter would end up in the same high school as his son? What a crazy Five-Year Party!

The point of the Five-Year Party—and of most of the exercises in this chapter—is to reinforce in both your conscious self and your subconscious mind that which you want to become reality. If you spend an evening "trying out" the lifestyle you want and deserve, you later begin to react to situations, and attract those people, that support your goal. Now, this is not witchcraft. You don't just have a party of this nature and then everything falls into place. But it does support your goal if you also take other necessary steps to accomplish them. Conversely, if you don't believe or trust that you can and will make it happen, you will remain stuck with you old lifestyle. For some women, living in an old comfort zone while clinging to their fear of change is exactly what keeps them from growing.

QUESTION

What goal—large or small—have you attained in the past that at first you thought was impossible to achieve?

Talking Your Way to a New Attitude

There's a compelling method of creating change that helps you trust and believe in your wishes. You know all about it—it's a common tool used today. It's called self-talk. We've hinted at this in earlier passages in this book. Self-talk is simply what you tell yourself day after day, and it's very powerful. Encouraging statements that you give yourself are also called affirmations. Many athletes, as well as those in the corporate world, use positive self-talk and affirmations to keep themselves in a productive place.

Our subconscious is a strong entity. Information and obscure memories are stored there, only to bubble up during the most surprising times. The messages we give ourselves get locked inside, and we then act upon those thoughts. Our beliefs determine our experience. Thoughts like "I'll never be rich" or a sentence you heard a long time ago, like "my life is over after forty" can awaken at any given moment and affect our actions today.

Here's the interesting thing about our subconscious: We can tell it something we want it to believe and it will absorb that new thought. No judgment—just acceptance. This is worth repeating: We can tell our subconscious something we want it to believe, and it will. We have to do it over and over again, because our subconscious likes familiar stuff. After a while our behavior changes. If every day you woke up and said to yourself, "I've got so much to do today, I don't know if I can handle it," what effect do you think it would have? We'll tell you: You'd carry the sense that you're struggling throughout the day. Every day. Same thing if you're always giving credence to your stress. Constantly thinking, "I'm so stressed" keeps you tense and uncomfortable. However, you have a choice. You can alter your perception of your world. If you activate different, positive thoughts (without necessarily believing them, mind you) and put new words into your subconscious, like "I can handle it" or, even better, "I thrive on this," you can improve your day tenfold. Misery is optional. But you already know that.

Now that you understand that you can reprogram your thoughts with your own brand of self-talk, the first step is discovering what you normally say to yourself. This breakthrough is important. We set ourselves up for failure all the time. The other day a woman said to us, "I'm getting so many new ideas I can't keep up with them." We quickly reminded her to give her subconscious the message that of course she could handle it all, that she loves all the new ideas coming to her. Once you realize what you're saying, change it. Simply replace those words. Your subconscious doesn't filter or judge what you're dispensing, and you honestly don't have to believe the newly programmed thought; you just have to keep saying it to yourself. If you say, "I'm happy" several times every day, we guarantee that you will find yourself cheerful more often than not. One important note here: Program your words using only the present tense. If your subconscious receives "I will be happy," it assumes that this feeling will happen sometime in the future. Phrases like "I will be rolling in money" won't serve you well, either. If, on the other hand, you say, "I am abundant. I'm paying off all the bills, taking fun vacations, and feeling happy and content," adding as many details as you can, your subconscious will start to believe it, your actions will support it, and before you know it you'll be experiencing a shift in your reality. No, it's not magic. No, you can't just sit around and wish for things. However, you can change your perception of a situation, and your creative mind will help you think of ways to have your dream become a reality. Don't take this lightly; it really works.

From Thought to Paper

Another highly effective exercise for changing your perception in order to have it work toward your happiness is writing it down. Just like the five-year party and self-talk, if you actually put your goal down on paper and write—in detail and in the present tense, as if it's really happening—you will automatically begin to attract those things and those people that will support your particular goal. It doesn't happen overnight. It happens in its own time. But it will become a reality.

Marilyn has been doing this for almost thirty years:

> People often say I live a charmed life. And it is pretty good, but I always have to work at it. I am so grateful I have these tools to help me.
>
> I first learned this powerful strategy in the early seventies from a man who later became my brother-in-law. He taught me to be diligent about keeping my writing in the present tense and to write as many details as I could. After a while I found it extremely helpful to add little drawings. I would draw my family in a loving circle with lots of money around us, or on a dream vacation, or buying a new house. If you looked at my old dream book you would be amazed at all the things that have come true. Even the birth of my daughter. Listen, it was a big deal back then, because many years before I had asked my husband to get a vasectomy, and he had complied. When I wrote and drew myself holding my baby daughter in my goal book, he needed to get that thing reversed, I needed to conceive, and the timing had to be such as to produce a girl. As I mentioned earlier in the book, she's now sixteen.
>
> In the eighties my belief in this process was reinforced by a tape given to me by a good friend. It was a fascinating motivational tape from speaker and author Mark Victor Hansen. One of the strategies he advocated was adding at the bottom of every page in your dream book these commanding words: "This or something *better* is manifesting itself for the good of all concerned." That little prayer made me feel like I could then let go of my worries regarding that particular goal and trust that it would happen in a way even better than I could imagine.
>
> To this day I continue to do this exercise. I'm sure it played a

big part in what got me here—writing a second book and having a wonderful, loving family around me to support and fuel my goals.

The first part of setting goals is getting organized. Sometimes that starts with a list. Here's Gina's encouraging story:

It just happened last week—I got fired up and excited about life again! Did a miracle occur? No. A plan came together. After six months of wandering aimlessly, I set a goal. First, the background:

After a long (twenty-two years!) and successful career as an executive in the corporate world, I was at a career crossroads. Though my enthusiasm for the job at hand had been slipping for a few years, and I was complaining more and more about the politics of it all, I had never considered another profession. But then, I hadn't been out of work and *forced to reevaluate my career path.*

I'm a bit embarrassed to tell you how the revelation and goal setting came about, because it's so simple. I just made a list. I made a list of all the things I enjoy, from spending time with animals to reading to producing live events to house renovations and interior design. Then I went back over the list to determine if any of those areas could translate to a fulfilling career that would provide a comfortable income. *Ding, ding, ding*—house renovation and interior design! Creatively decorating a room! I can do that! What about all those big events I've produced? I realized that I needed more than "good taste." I needed formal training.

I talked to people. My research included calling three interior designers and "interviewing" them about the joys of creating beautiful and comforting living spaces; contacting the School of Interior Design to find out about its programs; and breaking down my goal into manageable sections.

The most important questions I asked myself were: Can you

see yourself doing it? And do you have passion for it? A resounding "yes" to both questions! Decision made!

I know that the process of changing careers won't be easy—I've got two and a half years of school ahead of me. But I have a goal. A direction. And I imagine that my passion for interior design and my excitement at reinventing myself will carry me through. And sometimes when the going gets tough, I'll just have to remind myself: I can do this—I have been successful before and I will be again.

(It doesn't hurt that all of my friends are cheering me on!)

ACTIVITY: One, Two, Three

1. Following Gina's simple but effective list idea, write down all the things you enjoy.
2. Next, go back over the list to determine if any of those areas can translate to a fulfilling career that would provide a comfortable income.
3. Do a little research on the topic. Call and interview people. Find out where you might get some training.

Another way to stay encouraged about setting future goals is to take a good look at the ones you've attained *in just the last year.* You can do this any time of the year. Get together and create a ritual, an alternative to the New Year's resolutions so many people make (and break) each year. Here are Nancy's thoughts:

Both Marilyn and I are believers in the power of ritual. We bring candles, sage, pen, and paper into a safe, familiar environment. It starts with us writing down the important events that shaped our lives during the past year and how we handled them. We sit in silence and reflect on our amazing achievements. Some things we set out to do, like putting on an art exhibit; others simply came up during the year, like facing the death of a family pet or letting go of anger toward a coworker. We read our lists to each other, giving each item the reverence it deserves, and then we pat each other on the back for the courage, fortitude, or determination used to complete our goals. We are always amazed at what we have done!

We light a candle and say a prayer for the past year and give thanks for it. Next, we burn the sage to "clear" the air for the coming year. Then we write our list for the new year—our dreams and hopes. We always remember to take out the "should"s, and we remind each other to write what is in our hearts. We read our lists to each other and then prioritize them. The candle for the new year is lit, and a heartfelt prayer of thanks is said, always ending with the now famous "This or something better is manifesting itself for the good of all concerned."

This ritual has become my favorite part of the New Year holiday: a time of reflection and an expression of gratitude, shared with a friend I love—and whose support has helped me achieve my wildest dreams!

ACTIVITY: Just in One Year

Use the template Marilyn and Nancy use to help yourself gain perspective on the things you have accomplished in the last year. Sometimes it helps to have your calendar with you to spark your memory.

- Begin by thinking about the date one year ago.
- List all the important obstacles you've faced and gotten past during that time period.
- List any surprises that have come your way that you have handled. Explain how that came about.
- List any goals you wanted that now have been achieved.
- Take turns reading your items out loud. Be sure to point out what it took for that person to make it through the obstacle and give her the proper congratulations.

- Light the sage and say a respectful good-bye to that part of your life.
- Write down the goals you want to achieve this next year.
- Share them with your group.
- Light a candle and "bless" your intentions.

Seven Daily Steps to Reach Your Goals

Life coach Sharon Childers gave us a formula she often uses with her clients regarding keeping goals.

1. Create a compelling vision of your success and visualize it for ten minutes every morning.
2. Throughout the day, record all your inspired ideas and actions.
3. Script your day before you start it.
   How you want to feel
   Ideal experiences you want to have
   What you want to create, attract, or achieve today
4. In the morning, record five things you want to accomplish today.
5. In the evening, list your results and your feelings and thoughts about them.
6. Before bedtime, read the statement you've written about the goal you want to achieve, focus your attention on what is working, and think about the positive aspects of your day. Write all this in your journal and notice evidence of your manifestations.
7. Have fun with all these steps!

If you're having a tough time thinking of some daily goals, here are a few to get you started:

1. Let go of the past: Today I'm going to keep the past where it belongs—in the past. I'm concentrating on what's important to me today and how I want to use my actions to create a happy tomorrow.

2. Appreciate your mate: Today I am letting go of the irritations that naturally come with living with another person. I appreciate my _______________ for the little thing he/she does. I love his/her ______________________. These are the things I choose to focus on today.
3. Get healthy, stay healthy: All day today I'm choosing food, activities, and company that will keep me healthy.
4. Make one person happy today: I'm looking for an opportunity to make at least one other person happy today.

Creative Visualization: There's a Safe Place to Go

When we're faced with making big changes in our lives, we can feel anxious. Sometimes it's easier to live with discontentment and restlessness than to face the stress of change. Every time we push through those feelings and grow emotionally, we are so much more happy. To help you confront change, you can create a safe place in your mind that will always be there to comfort you, especially during the stress of change.

The following meditation is designed to comfort you in times of emotional distress. It is derived from a meditation that Nancy experienced many years ago when she attended a healing retreat at Glastonbury Abbey.

Begin by lighting a candle. Take three deep breaths and watch the flame glow. This candle symbolizes your spirit. As you focus on the light of the candle, imagine it as your spirit, a spirit that is everlasting. Remember that your spirit, like the flame of the candle, continues to burn inside of you, no matter what happens in the external, material world. There is nothing in the world that can destroy this light that burns in you—no problem, no sickness, not even death. It is an everlasting flame, your spirit. It is your soul—the soul of a strong woman.

As you look into the flame, think back to a time when you were a child. Picture yourself as this little girl. Picture what you might be wearing, what your hair looked like, and the things you liked to play with. Think of a moment in your life when you were a happy, innocent, and carefree child. What a pretty little girl you are! Right now your world is a place of endless possibilities, just waiting for you to explore.

Is there a special place where you feel the happiest? Think about where that might be. Is it your room? Your backyard? A secret place you share with your friends? If you don't yet have a picture, make one up. Create a warm, safe environment—one that a little girl might love to visit. It's your secret place, a place where you are the happiest and safest little girl in the whole world.

Maybe there's someone special with you as well. It might be your mother or father, a grandparent, or your closest friend. It could be an angel or someone famous who seems like they would be safe and nurturing. Imagine them with you in your special place. They are holding your hand. Doesn't it feel good? Sit with them for a while, and simply be. Nothing can harm you in this safe place. You can come back here and visit whenever you want—it's yours. Nothing can take it away from you.

Remember this little image whenever you feel worried about your future. Let the child in you feel protected. You can go there whenever you want—even if it's for just a second or two, waiting at a red light, preparing a meal, or walking to the parking lot—anytime. Give yourself this gift often. It's your safe place, and it's always there to comfort you.

ACTIVITY: First Half, Second Half

Picture yourself as the leading character in a play or novel. Write a paragraph that describes your life so far in very positive terms. For example, if you grew up as the child of an alcoholic parent but have learned many life lessons from that experience, write that as part of the description.

Now add a second paragraph that depicts the second half of your life, as you would like to live it in the future. Reread the two paragraphs and at the end of them repeat this mantra to yourself: "My life is unfolding just as I want it to."

~

There are many more practical ways to set your sights on a goal and achieve it. We suspect there's a strong possibility that you already know countless ways to do this, and it's also possible that you have let the little things in life stop you. This chapter was created to remind you to clear out your negative thoughts with affirmative self-talk, journal writing, and visualizations (like the Five-Year Party). See yourself trying something new and enjoying it in ways you've never before experienced. Have fun creating a night and morning fantasy. Don't let life's little things get in the way of your goals.

The following chapter—"Get a Coach"—will show you how to get the support you need to follow through on your plans.

Chapter Nine

Turning Point No. 9: Get a Coach

YOUR MOTHER'S MIDLIFE: *While our mothers may have had plenty of support in raising their families, they rarely had support when it came to fulfilling their dreams once they reached midlife. By the time a woman of our mothers' generation reached fifty, she'd resigned herself to life as she knew it, feeling that it was "too late" to make a change. If she was ahead of her time and forged ahead, she most likely didn't receive much support from the outside world.*

YOUR MIDLIFE: *In order for the world to change its perception of aging women, we have to make a commitment to changing our perception of ourselves. Once we have done that, we need to surround ourselves with a support system to put our new beliefs into action. One of the best ways to do that is to get a coach.*

"Girl power" is a term found in the vocabulary of most young women of today. Being midlifers, we can't remember if it originated with the Spice Girls or the Powerpuff Girls—but it doesn't matter, because the term has a strong message. One woman alone can be hardworking and tenacious; two women with the same intention create power. With the support of like-minded women, we can achieve almost anything. One of the tools we introduced you to earlier was the "midlife connection," asking you to form a Fearless Aging Club while reading this workbook. We know that girl power really works—now we are going to ask you to take that concept a step further.

Coaching—Not Just for Athletes

There is a new breed of "therapist" available to us these days. They call themselves "life coaches." Some people pay big money to get their specific kind of counsel. And as with therapists, you have to find the one who is a right fit for you. A life coach will help you organize your priorities and make solid goals and will then hold you accountable to follow through on them. They sort of do for your life plan what a personal trainer does for your exercise plan: keep you going when you're tempted to fall back on old, lazy habits. A life coach can see your dreams and future goals through new eyes and help you get over the usual—and sometimes unusual—bumps in the road.

Another way to get this style of assistance is for you and a girlfriend to agree to help each other—as a life coach would. This is different from the kind of support a friend would normally generously give another. This is a commitment to each other.

Nancy realized that she and Marilyn had performed the role of coach for each other over the course of the past few years:

> I wouldn't have accomplished half of the goals I set for myself if not for Marilyn urging me forward, inspiring me, and sometimes downright goading me on (especially in the area of writing, where I had a block before I even had a flow!). It started out as an informal arrangement in which we encouraged each other to set and achieve goals. We then decided to try an experiment: What if we took this arrangement seriously, as if each of us were paying the other to mentor and motivate her?
>
> First, we identified goals (regarding our art and writing) and wrote them down. Using my fax machine, we made two copies—one to keep posted for ourselves, and one for our "coach." Next, we set up a weekly schedule that we promised to adhere to. We touched base with each other every day by phone or e-mail.
>
> When Marilyn was more productive than I was, it had the

effect of motivating me to do more, and vice versa. She had worked on a new chapter while I had been slacking? Well, I had better sit down and work. If I started a new oil painting, she couldn't wait to catch up. It's amazing what a little healthy competition among friends can bring about.

The results? One year later we had completed some twenty oil paintings each, exhibited our work in a gallery, written a book proposal, and completed two-thirds of a manuscript. Because of our commitment to helping each other achieve these goals, distant dreams became reality.

We developed the following guidelines based on our own coaching relationship:

1. Select a friend who seems to have the kind of energy and outlook that you do. While it's not necessary for her to have the same goal, a commitment to the process is necessary. Geographical proximity is not a requirement, as you can work via e-mail or telephone.
2. Set up an initial goal-setting session, a time in which you will brainstorm with each other about what you hope to accomplish. List your goals and post them in a place where you will look at them frequently, like on your desk or taped to your computer (or maybe on your refrigerator?).
3. Establish regularly scheduled "check-in" times (at minimum, once a week) with your coach in which you will give each other progress reports. Hold each other accountable, and if one of you falls behind in a goal, the other one should help her determine what's blocking her.
4. Decide on a time frame for achieving your goals (three months is the minimum). Set a meeting for that date to evaluate how you've done and where you want to go from here. You may want to draw up a list of new goals or continue to work on your current ones.

Professional Advice

We asked professional coach Sharon Childers of Life Harmonics transformational coaching for her advice in entering into this arrangement with a friend. Here is what she recommends:

> If you are interested in coaching a friend, it is a good idea to understand what a coach is and what you need to keep in mind if you are going to put yourself into that role.
>
> What is a coach? A coach is someone who inspires people to reach their fullest potential. Coaches see their clients as experts in their own personal and professional lives. A coach comes from the perspective of seeing their client as creative, resourceful, and whole. Coaches don't fix their clients. The coach inspires and facilitates self-discovery and helps their clients stay responsible and accountable for their own commitments. Coaches hold the highest vision for their clients and create a safe space for personal and professional growth and development.
>
> What is the difference between a coach, a therapist, and a consultant?
>
> Where therapists may diagnose or prescribe and focus on their patients' past issues and problems, coaches focus on the present and the future. They are partners with their clients and on an equal level. A coach's focus with the client is on moving forward and taking action and is a co-creative proactive experience.
>
> A consultant is usually hired for a specific project and is more attached to a specific outcome. A consultant is also there to deal with the symptoms, come up with the solutions, and either tell the client what to do or actually do it for the client. Coaches inspire their clients to come up with their own solutions. A coach is more of a facilitator in a process.

Sharon also gave us ten points that anyone who wants to play the role of coaching a friend should be aware of.

1. First you have to establish and set certain agreements and commitments, including session times, amount of weeks or months you agree to be coach, and, most importantly, the time or money exchange between the two parties involved.
2. You need to create a level of intimacy, trust, and safety in the coaching relationship.
3. You need to be an active listener in the session, staying present and undistracted, giving your full attention, and listening for themes and patterns that may need to be addressed.
4. You should ask powerful, thought-provoking questions that will make your friend stretch and grow and help her find her own answers and solutions.
5. You need to maintain integrity, honesty, and sincerity.
6. You should provide ongoing support for new behaviors and new actions—for instance, helping your friend push through fears and take risks.
7. You should always ask permission to coach a friend in new areas and on sensitive issues.
8. You need to demonstrate respect for personal learning styles. Some people are more auditory, some more visual, and some more kinesthetic. You can offer information in different ways to best serve your friend.
9. You should see your friend as a partner in this process; you are both working on a level playing field.
10. You must always show concern for the well-being of your friend.

If you decide to coach a friend or have a friend coach you, it is crucial that you designate specific times for the sessions. Be very clear when you are putting on your "coaching hat." At the beginning of each session, the coach should set an intention with the friend for the session. To gain greater clarity, focus on what is working and also look at what is not working. If either friend feels that the coaching process is not working for her for whatever reason, she should let her partner know; both parties should agree beforehand not to hold any grudges in this eventuality. It would be a good idea to try the coaching arrangement on a trial basis for a month to see if you can work together in these roles.

You can contact Sharon for more information about coaching at her Web site, www.lifeharmonics.com.

QUESTIONS:

What areas of your life could benefit most from working with a coach?

Complete the following statement with the first thing that comes to mind: "If I had a coach, I would be able to accomplish ________________."

Creative Visualization: Your Support Team

(NUMBER NINE ON CD)

What do you think would happen if you had the support of some of the "greats" on your team? What if you could get advice about self-determination from Rosa Parks, suggestions about how to be open to your imagination from Walt Disney, opinions regarding compassion from Maya Angelou, and total support from Oprah Winfrey? If you were to have a "board of directors" meeting regarding you and your goals, who would you want on your team? Would it be any of those people mentioned, or maybe one of your favorite teachers, a neighbor from your childhood, Alex Trebek, or your sister? Think about that as we do the next guided visualization.

Get into a comfortable position, either sitting in a chair, lying down, or cross-legged on the floor. Close your eyes. Begin to inhale through your nostrils and exhale through your mouth, gradually intensifying the deepness of your breath. With each inhalation, expand your stomach and chest, filling your lungs with air, and with each exhalation, empty your breath from your chest and stomach until they feel "collapsed." Do this very slowly. Breathe in through your nose to the count of four, hold your breath to the count of seven, then slowly exhale from your mouth to the count of eight. With each new breath imagine yourself pulling in positive energy and everything you need, and with each exhalation feel yourself letting go of negativity and everything you don't need in your life. Do this several times.

Imagine that you are walking into a room where there's a board meeting going on. Five people are sitting in soft, plush business chairs around a beautiful walnut table. On the table there's a lit candle, a decorated box, and a brass plaque that reads THINK TANK. In front of each chair is a piece of paper and a beautiful pen. You see an empty chair waiting for you. Sit in your chair and look around the table. Who is on your support team? It can be anyone you want. Think of the kind of energy, strength, and comfort each person brings to the team. You take one another's hands and create a circle of support. A moment passes, and someone gets a good idea. They write it down on the paper and then put it in the box. Your teammate looks at you and says, "This is for you—when you are ready, you can just reach in the box and get it. You will always have me on your team." Thank them for being there for you. Each team member takes a turn writing down a good idea and putting it in the box. Each time they do it you tell them how grateful you are to have their support. You once again grab one another's hands. You all bow your heads and say in unison, "So be it." You blow out the candle and take the box home with you.

In a moment you are going to come back to the present, feeling relaxed and refreshed. Begin by taking three deep breaths. Notice the outside sounds. Start to wiggle your fingertips and your toes. Breathing regularly, open your eyes.

Share

Don't forget to process this visualization with your group or a friend or write about it in a journal. Who was on the team? What was written on the sheets of paper?

~

When you allow yourself to dream, when you visualize yourself doing a new activity, when you tell yourself you can do it, when you muster up courage to follow your dream, when you open yourself up to new possibilities, and when you ask for help, you will manifest a new and exhilarating life. It will take some time for you to learn the new "job" and probably ten years or more for you to get bored with this wonderful, stimulating way of living. Go for it. And then become someone's muse.

Chapter Ten

Turning Point No. 10: Awaken to the Muse

YOUR MOTHER'S MIDLIFE: *There have always been fabulous older women in the world—but in our mothers' midlife they were rarely acknowledged or accorded their rightful place as our role models, mentors, and muses.*

YOUR MIDLIFE: *Have a champion, and be someone's champion. Today we can freely worship them—those trailblazing older women who motivate us, inspire us, and remind us that we can truly be fantastic at any age. Identify your muse and emulate her. The most important quality she possesses is wisdom—and that is something that comes only with years of living.*

The older women you admire can offer important insights into the woman you are capable of becoming. They can also provide you with a source of inspiration and encouragement, serving as a reminder of the possibilities that are out there when we work to achieve a dream. We like to call them our muses, a word that comes from the myth of the sister goddesses of Ancient Greece. They were the nine daughters of Zeus and Mnemosyne who presided over the various arts. *Muse* came to be the term for a woman who inspires an artist or a poet.

Let a muse inspire you to make your life a work of art. The first step is to identify your muse. Muses can be famous or unknown, deceased or alive, and of any origin. Think of those unique role models in life. Who are the women whose qualities you most admire? Remember, they don't have to be famous. Mothers, grandmothers, aunts, teachers—recall the women you admired for their inner grace. The most important quality our version of muse must possess is the capability to inspire you to age beautifully.

~

Ilene explains what makes her muse so important to her:

> When my wonderful friend Anne Katzky turned eighty-five, I was lucky enough to be considered one of her best girlfriends at her birthday lunch. I first met Anne through a children's charity. She has become my muse because she defies heartbreak and pain. She gives to the world so much more than she takes.
>
> Anne had a very tough childhood, then endured a difficult time in her life when she had to send her own children to live in foster care because she couldn't provide for them, and yet she bounced back stronger than she thought she could ever be. She's a whirlwind of energy, passion, and smarts. She is involved with more worthwhile organizations than you can imagine—ones that directly benefit children.
>
> She's also my style muse! I've never seen her without her false lashes, perfectly coifed hair, adorable outfit, and sparkly jewelry.
>
> Being with Anne always makes me feel good because she shows her friends how treasured they are. If I can be half the woman she is, I'll be amazing.

Ilene's muse has shown her that an eighty-five-year-old woman can be awe-inspiring. Shouldn't we all aspire to become someone like Anne Katzky rather than wasting precious energy worrying about aging?

QUESTION

Name two women over sixty-five whom you admire. What is it about them that you love? What qualities do you have in common with them?

Inspiration

Having a unique grande dame in your life might lead you to follow in her path someday. Fifty-one-year-old Pauline is originally from El Salvador, where she was exposed to her true muse:

> We call her Tia Chipi. I have a strong memory of when I was very young and I used to go to her house. She would be painting a mural—a peach tree with peaches on it. It was the most amazing thing I had witnessed, and I wanted to be like her. She was not like the rest of high-society women, concerned with her appearance—she always had paint on her clothing and in her hair. She was a little bitty thing—sort of a small version of Diane Sawyer in looks—and though she never combed her hair or wore makeup, she was received and admired in the homes of the very wealthy. She was very intelligent and could hold a conversation with anyone. She loved history and art.
>
> Her pets included a puma, a monkey, and some dogs, and for a while she emptied her pool and kept a deer in it. There were always surprises at her home. The servants sat down at the same table as her for meals, which was unheard of everywhere else. She was always thinking of designs and ideas, twirling her hair as she thought. She even had her own museum of Mayan Indian pottery, which she let me photograph for a special studies class I took in 1965. She took interest in my art and brought me to small Indian villages to visit local potters. I loved Tia Chipi. She was my idol. Her sometimes bizarre, always unique lifestyle was bursting with creativity and joy. She helped me become the artist I am now.

Who has the courage to be as wild as Tia Chipi? Some of you would love to have paint in your hair and a deer in your swimming pool. Others might find inspiration from the next two women.

Look to Your Past

Like Pauline, maybe your muse is in your own backyard or your own family. Nancy's grandmothers had a powerful influence on her life.

> I want to be like my two wonderful grandmothers, who were strong matriarchs of the family. Their husbands having died decades before them, they were the undisputed leaders of their clans.
>
> My mother's mother, Gertrude Rousseau, was the kind of woman who, in the course of a day, could bake a perfect peach pie, embroider a hunt scene, roast a pheasant, chop the head off an errant copperhead when gardening—all while tending to a house full of children and grandchildren. She was strong and feminine all at once, an iron-willed woman dressed in lace and pearls. She is the epitome of who I want to be. When she was well into her seventies I asked her if she would ever consider plastic surgery. Her response inspired this poem:
>
> *My brothers and I somersault down the hill your house sits on,*
> *Smearing grass and gnats.*
> *Seersucker uniforms camouflaged green,*
> *We return to you*
> *To be stripped and scrubbed*
> *Into pure, sexless children.*
>
> *By my bed in a rocker*
> *You sing me a lullaby,*
> *Your silver hair undone around your shoulders,*
> *more beautiful than a bride's.*

Yesterday, pointing to the lines on your face,
You said, "These I got from worrying about your grandfather,
and these I got from laughing with him."
We were standing in the garden
Looking for bean sprouts.

And then there was Diddy. I've mentioned her several times throughout this book because to me she was a living saint of a woman. She was my father's mother, Elizabeth Hester Alspaugh. Her home was a giant playhouse, with a banister to slide down, a piano to bang on, and a closet always open for playing dress-up. She saw the best in everyone; the story goes that once someone said she would find good in the devil. She replied, "Well, someone has to do his job."

After her seven children were grown, she took in boarders at her big rambling house, and her army of grandchildren were constant visitors.

There was scary old Mr. Koontz, a traveling salesman who lived upstairs, and the virile young mechanic Jesse, who lived in the basement apartment. One day my cousins and I trespassed into his room, delighted to find an array of *Playboy* centerfolds adorning the cinder-block walls. Knowing we wouldn't be punished, we reported his sins to Diddy. Her only comment was "Why, I think it's wonderful the young man has an appreciation of the beauty of the female form."

The Diddy stories are endless, and though she's been gone for twenty years, my cousins, aunts, and uncles keep her memory alive by having "Diddy parties," where we share our favorite moments from her life. She would have loved that legacy.

What qualities do Nancy's grandmothers possess that are close to your strengths? What would you like to build on?

ACTIVITY: The Muse Quiz

The following little thought-provoking quiz circulated over the Internet a few years ago. Take it and see how you do.

Part I

1. Name the five wealthiest women in the world.
2. Name the last five female U.S. Open winners.
3. Name the last five winners of the Miss America contest.
4. Name ten women who have won the Nobel or Pulitzer Prize.
5. Name the last half-dozen Academy Award winners for best actress.

How did you do?

The point is, none of us remember the headliners of yesterday. These are no second-rate achievers. They are the best in their fields. But the applause dies. Awards tarnish. Achievements are forgotten. Accolades and certificates are buried with their owners.

Part II

1. List a few teachers who aided your journey through school.
2. Name three friends who have helped you through a difficult time.
3. Name five people who have taught you something worthwhile.
4. Think of a few people who have made you feel appreciated and special.
5. Think of five people you enjoy spending time with.
6. Name a half-dozen heroes whose stories have inspired you.

Easier? The lesson here is that the people who make a difference in your life are not the ones with the most credentials, the most money, or the most awards.

~

If your muse is a well-known figure and you have the opportunity to see her in person, go for it! You might be surprised at the results.

Nancy and a friend went in search of the legendary artist and potter Beatrice Woods several years ago. They found the ninety-nine-year-old sari-clad artist holding court in her studio, and she graciously showed them her latest work. Before they left her, they were compelled to ask this woman, who had once been the lover of many famous men, including the bohemian French artist Marcel Duchamp, what she would do differently in her life if she were to live it all over again. After reflecting on the question a moment or two she answered:

"More belly dancing, my dears. If I had it to do all over again, I'd do more belly dancing."

To this day, Nancy hears those words whenever she starts taking life too seriously.

~

Marilyn also had an opportunity to meet a muse and found out an important rule.

DON'T PISS OFF YOUR MUSE

About ten years ago when I lived in northern California, I would take a daily walk that meandered through some neighborhoods and wound up alongside a creek. Sometimes I have superstitious leanings; back then I had somehow determined that as soon as I hit the creek path, there would be signs from the universe. It was up to me to interpret the lesson. I know I'm a little out there, but what the hell—it's who I am.

I'd be walking along, round the corner, and run right into a sign. For a while it was the pods, which had dropped from the eucalyptus trees. It was challenging to walk on them, so I had to create my own safe path. I looked at this as a metaphor for life—that sometimes it's difficult, but you have to make your own way. I had a tree that "spoke" to me. I called it "Tree of Support," and I would think of all the ways in which I receive and give support. Like I said, once I rounded the corner and stepped onto the path, signs appeared.

One day I was in deep thought about my pending move to Los Angeles. I was worried about making such a huge change in my life. I rounded the corner and saw an old woman. I thought, "Sign. Big sign coming up." She was wearing an old sweater; each buttonhole had a large safety pin keeping it closed. She startled when she saw me and for some odd reason blurted out, "I was sick for most of my life—till 'the change of life.' After that I was as healthy as I could be." Then she turned away and walked toward an old house sandwiched between new suburban ones. Wow! My busy mind went to work. . . . "The *change!* This must mean that when I move I'll feel better than ever!"

The following weeks I hoped to see her again and get some more wisdom, but no one was there. I really wanted one more piece of sage advice before I moved. I bought a sweater with snaps instead of buttons and brought it along to give to her; I'd decided to knock on her door and, hopefully, hang on to every word she said to me.

I walked up her sidewalk with anticipation. I knocked a few times, and she finally answered. She took one look at me with my little gift and started to yell. "How did you know where I live? How dare you trespass. Who the hell invited you anyway?" She was pissy. My muse was real pissy. I gave her the sweater anyway—she was barely grateful. She kept barking at me till I turned around and left.

What did I learn from the universe that time? *Don't get greedy.* She had said everything I needed to learn, and I should have simply been grateful for that. Oh, and don't piss off your muse.

Jan learned from her old Brownie leader that some rules are made to be broken. She has carried the leader's spunky attitude with her ever since childhood. Read the next passage and see if this is the kind of muse you would aspire to become.

BREAKING RULES

One of my earliest and best role models was my Brownie troop leader, an incredible woman named Jane Williams. She was interested in saving the environment even in the fifties, back when everyone else thought that nature was infinitely and effortlessly renewable, ours for the taking.

One day when she was leading her troop of Brownies on a woodland hike we passed a piece of land marked off with barbed-wire fence and No Trespassing signs. Mrs. Williams spotted a dead fawn and thought it presented a perfect opportunity to discuss the cycle of life.

Unfortunately, we couldn't get close enough to the fawn to see all she wanted to show us, so she whipped out a pair of wire cutters. As she was about to snip the barbed wire, our little troop started chorusing like baby robins under crow attack. "Mrs. Williams! Mrs. Williams! The sign! The sign!"

The No Trespassing sign was clearly visible and no more than a dozen feet away. Mrs. Williams looked straight at it.

"Sign?" she asked. "What sign?" And she cut right through the fence. "Come, girls!"

We were astonished. We'd never seen anyone blatantly break the law like that. Unfazed, Mrs. Williams marched us over to the dead fawn, pointing out the bugs that were eating it, who would in their own turn die and restore the fawn's nutrients to the earth. Dust to dust in graphic detail. Then she made us gather up the fawn—bugs and all—and take it home. She taught us how to skin it, gut it, and boil it down to its skeleton. We spent the next winter reassembling it to the last little bone. By the end, every single one of us knew exactly how a deer is built plus all the words to that "knee bone connected to the thighbone" song.

I also learned that, for a good reason, nice women can break the rules.

Over the years, Mrs. Williams broke more rules—rules that said women could not have an effect. She lobbied her representatives in the state and federal government to clean up Wisconsin's environment and raised money to create a wilderness preserve, which today gives thousands of people an understanding of nature like the one Mrs. Williams once gave us. She's in her late seventies now, but she's still going strong. Most recently, she's turned her sunroom into a hospital for wounded owls, eagles, and hawks.

Through the years, I've carried her lessons in boldness with me, used them when necessary, and passed them on wherever possible. Sign? What sign? Come, girls!

There's an old saying: "You may be only one person in the world, but you may also be the world to one person." Once you identify who your muse is and see the qualities you want to emulate, begin blazing your own trail and share your wisdom (which you now have) with those who are open and attracted to your energy. Suzy has the right idea.

THE MUSE AND HER NEPHEW

My brother's son is twenty-three, with all that that implies. Newly graduated and living alone in a city for the first time, he's come to me. Raised in the suburbs, he doesn't quite know what to make of things. He is responsible, and although I suspect he drinks too much, who cares—we all did at that age. The troubling issue he seems to be struggling with is his headlong determination to make a boatload of money and equip himself with all of the trappings that this culture demands. It is hard to stop and just take a breath when you are that age, so telling him to slow down and not stress himself with this competitive rush is difficult. It's a strange feeling to have the wisdom to both see the bumps in his road and understand that he's too young to take advice about how to avoid them; and it's nice to reside in the faith that he'll find his own way. I like this place. I don't have to parent this wonderful young man; I just have to give him one of my warm smiles and remind him that he's doing fine.

I was always the "crazy aunt," the multimarried bad example not to emulate. Yet, like a moth to the flame, this young man sought me out. I had to ask myself why. It's not just cause I'm a relative and I make good pasta. I think he feels relaxed with me, and I think his loneliness may have compelled him. Hillary said it takes a village. The Lord knows that ain't original with her; I expect the Aborigines could show her a thing or two. But she is right. I feel that I can be of some comfort to him, that I can offer humor and provide a place where he can be himself. And I get a new friend in the bargain.

The irony of being a teacher is that you never realize the true effect on your students. Not until years later do you realize that your fifth-grade teacher, Mrs. Sweeney, taught you the meaning of sharing. Of course, she is long dead and you can't call her up to say how grateful you are. What you can do is pass on your gift.

Creative Visualization: The Interview

(NUMBER TEN ON CD)

This visualization is meant to help you see that there's plenty of time left to do the things you need to do. It lets you see how quickly time goes by and serves as a wake-up call to make your life into what you want. It can also bring you to a place of gratitude for who you are now.

Get into a comfortable position, either sitting in a chair, lying down, or sitting cross-legged on the floor. Begin to inhale and exhale, gradually intensifying the deepness of your breath through your nostrils.

With each inhale, expand your stomach and chest, filling up your lungs with air, and with each exhale, empty your breath from your chest and stomach through your mouth until they feel "collapsed". Do this very slowly.

Breathe in through your nose to the count of four, hold your breath to the count of seven, and slowly exhale from your mouth for a count of eight. In 1-2-3-4. Hold 1-2-3-4-5-6-7. Exhale 1-2-3-4-5-6-7-8. With each new breath imagine yourself breathing in relaxation, and with each exhale feel yourself letting go of negativity. Inhale 1-2-3-4. Hold 1-2-3-4-5-6-7. Exhale 1-2-3-4-5-6-7-8. Do this several times.

Imagine how it would be if you would release the muscles in your jaw. Conjure up the sensation of letting go of all the tension you might be holding in your jaw. Feel the release. Now your facial muscles. Feel the tension going out of those muscle groups. Let your forehead relax. Let your eyes relax. Inhale 1-2-3-4. Hold 1-2-3-4-5-6-7. Exhale 1-2-3-4-5-6-7-8.

Now let your shoulders relax. Let the tension fade away from your neck and your shoulders. Take another deep breath and with the exhale, release and relax all the muscles in your neck and shoulders.

Breathing regularly now.

As you slowly go down your body releasing tension, let your stomach relax, then your hips, and now your abdomen. Let your thighs melt into a limp state, now your shins, your ankles, and your feet.

Picture yourself in a comfortable place where you would watch television. Make it warm and cozy. You're interested in seeing a piece being shown on *Dateline* about some women who are about to turn one hundred. Stone Phillips is introducing the segment. He says that the producers have located five ninety-nine-year-old women who all say they have no regrets. It promises to be fascinating. You see the first woman and you love her. She is beautifully and completely wrinkled. She has an undeniable twinkle in her eyes.

As you watch the piece, you begin to realize that this woman has had many experiences. Not all were considered good—or happy—experiences. She tells the viewing audience that each and every experience helped her to learn important things like courage and compassion. We find out that her only son grew up to become a very powerful and benevolent person. When asked to give some parenting tips, this wonderful woman hesitates for a moment. And then giggles. She says, "You know, I only parented for eighteen years. It was such a short time. I can't remember." This little old incredible lady is wise and loving. The interviewer is amazed that a mother would have such a cavalier attitude about parenting. The old woman says, "It all seems so big and important at the time, but looking back at everything I've done, parenting is one of many important things."

The camera then comes to a nursing home. Another wrinkled woman sits smiling at her viewing audience. She also has a sense of wisdom emanating from her being. When the interviewer asks her how she handled stress over the years, she replies, "Stress? What you call stress—we call life. I just lived life as best as I could."

The camera is now approaching a front porch. It's a pristine white porch. There's yet another beautiful woman sitting in the rocking chair. Take a good look at this one. She glows from within. It's you—many years from now.

The reporter has a few questions for you. No problem—you have the answers.

First question: Did you do the things you wanted to do? You answer. Were you playful and joyous? Answer. Did you give something special to anyone? What are you most proud of? What helped you get through the hard stuff? Did you ever forgive that person who hurt you? Did you ever find your passion? Did you leave the world a better place? How? What advice would you like to give to the viewing audience?

The reporter thanks you and the show is concluded. Stone Phillips is especially proud of you.

In a moment you are going to come back to the present, feeling relaxed and very refreshed. Begin by taking three deep breaths. Notice the outside sounds. Start to wiggle your fingertips and wiggle your toes. Move your head a little. Breathing regularly, open your eyes. Stretch. Look around the room. Wide awake.

Share

Don't forget to process this visualization with your group or a friend or write about it in a journal. What were some of your answers?

ACTIVITY: Make a Muse Altar

Decide on a muse or two whom you would most like to emulate. Create a little space for icons, symbols, and photographs of them. Include books or biographies written about them and examples of their work if they are famous, or letters and pictures of them if they are not. Try to identify one picture that you feel best captures the spirit of your muse. Frame it and put it on your altar. Look at it every day. For years, articles in women's magazine have promoted the trick of cutting out a picture of a slender model and taping it to our refrigerator door as a visual motivation to lose weight. This is the same idea, just taken in a different direction. If we can be inspired by a photograph to get thinner thighs, we can also be inspired to become more creative, fulfilled women. Nancy chose a picture of Georgia O'Keeffe taken by her photographer husband, Alfred Stieglitz; it depicts a young Georgia in the desert holding one of her flower paintings. Nancy put the picture on her bedside table; beside it she placed a picture of her beloved grandmother Diddy, who lived life with the most joyful enthusiasm of anyone she has ever known. Marilyn keeps Rosa Parks's photo above her computer as a reminder of how one single woman can make a difference, start a movement, and change an entire country for the better.

~

So pick a few muses and enjoy their gifts, then work on becoming one yourself. You have more to offer than you first thought. Imagine what we all have to look forward to—not only accepting middle age, but accepting and celebrating what lies beyond it. And we're proving to the world that not only is it *not* your mother's midlife, it's not your mother's old age anymore, either.

Conclude with Us

A few final thoughts now that you are well on your way (at least ten weeks along, anyway!) into this journey of living midlife to the fullest. We are not naive enough to think that after reading our book you will have moved from a place of anxiety to a place where you think hot flashes are simply power surges. After all, midlife is just like the rest of life—a rather messy business, full of twists and turns and surprises. We hope we have given you some ammunition to battle the hardest ones with a newfound sense of courage and optimism, as well as the inspiration to cherish the rest.

One last question: **How are you going to make a difference?** Take your time and think about this. When we get outside of our own heads and create something good and uplifting for someone else, we can't help but stop feeling sorry for ourselves. Depression cannot remain in a person's psyche when that person is giving someone else hope. It's all about the legacy, baby. Once more: What will you do to make someone's world a better place?

Poet Marianne Williamson believes that as we let our own light shine, we give other people permission to do the same. It is in realizing our own power that we can change our old perception that we are less valuable as we age. Remember, this is the *middle* of your life.

There is still plenty of light left to shine. And in letting your own light shine, in honoring your own power, you can start to change the world. You still have plenty of time to travel, write a poem, reconnect with an old friend, make a new friend, start a new career, forgive someone, fall in love, become independent, change your face, have a baby, start an art colony, design homes, hold a crack baby, learn feng shui, meet your hero, become someone's hero, straighten your teeth, see a Broadway play, create a Broadway play, find the child you put up for adoption, write a novel, learn a new language, begin meditating, change a law, start a movement . . . make a difference.

Go forth and shine!

During the creation of this book the authors sent an e-mail of their ten steps to fearless aging to their friends hoping to find women who would resonate with the subject. They received many interesting responses and included them in this book to show women all over the world that they're not alone. At the completion of the book a black lace shawl was sent all over the states to each contributor and each had her photo taken in it. Below are photos of the beautiful, fearless contributors, ages thirty-eight to sixty-two, proving further that it's not your mother's midlife.

Katerina Monemvassitis, 42
Chapter 1

Dr. Riki Polycove
51
Chapter 2

Suzy Hunt
57
Chapter 2

Vicki Vyinello
55
Chapter 2

Bev Smith
51
Chapter 2

Jan Kimbrough
52
Chapter 2

JoAnne Farley
47
Chapter 2

Garland Waller
52
Chapter 2

Eva Almos
46
Chapter 2

Kathryn Kaufman Seay, 42
Chapter 2

Tina Sloan
60
Chapter 2

Catherine Williams
43
Chapter 4

Nadine Kavenaugh
45
Chapter 4

Barbara Thornton
50
Chapter 4

Therese Gamba
41
Chapter 4

Sherry (Boo) Capers
51
Chapter 4

Penny Ruekberg
42
Chapter 4

Carlton Ward
55
Chapter 5

Cheryl Pappas
48
Chapter 5

Lilka Areton
62
Chapter 7

Mary McCutcheon-Smith, 52
Chapter 7

Joanne Roberts
50
Chapter 7

Ana Paniagua
44
Chapter 7

Joelene Ashker
38
Chapter 7

Gina Brittle-Macky
44
Chapter 8

Sharon Childers
41
Chapter 9

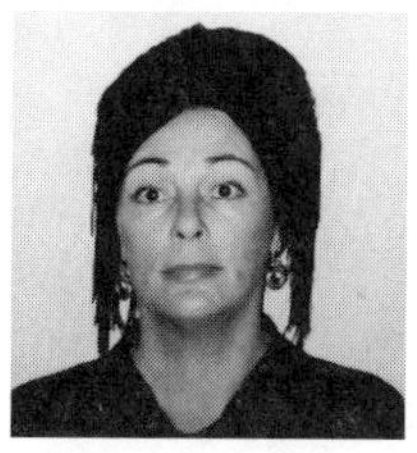
Pauline Lazzarini
52
Chapter 10

Ilene Graff
53
Chapter 10

Please visit our Web site at www.fearless-aging.com.